Top 30

Essential Short Stories in English:
1843 to 2000

Jim Knudsen

NAN'UN-DO

JN136680

Top 30
Essential Short Stories in English:
1843 to 2000

Copyright© 2019 by Jim Knudsen

All Rights Reserved

No part of this book may be reproduced in any form without written permission
from the author and Nan'un-do Co., Ltd.

To the Students

Top 30: Essential Short Stories in English: 1843 to 2000 introduces you to 30 wonderful short stories—30 of my favorites—written by some of the greatest authors in the English language. I am not a professional critic or literary scholar; I'm just a person who enjoys reading short fiction—and I thought it might be fun and useful to share that joy with you in some friendly, "chatty" mini-reviews. Of course, I do engage in a little "criticism," but it's all practical, positive, appreciative. My main goal is to try to pique your interest in each story by telling you a bit about its setting and plot and characters, pointing out a significant theme or two, citing a memorable passage, and presenting a comment here and there from writers and critics who love a story as much as I do and have something revealing or inspiring to say about it. This is all done with the hope that sometime, somewhere, you will want to read some of the stories on your own.

In choosing these stories, I have tried to give you a variety of styles, points of view, subject matter, settings, and author nationalities. In here you will find tales of adventure, mystery, romance, revenge, tragedy, and fantasy; stories that deal with marriage and family, social and political issues, history and traditions; stories written by authors from England, Ireland, Scotland, Canada, New Zealand, India, China, Poland, and the United States.

As for *Top 30*'s exercises, they were devised not to test, but to encourage deeper, more careful reading. Each activity asks you to go back to the text to look for key words, key details, key ideas, and then to write them down. I am confident that in the process, your vocabulary will become bigger and better, and your writing, reading, and listening skills will all greatly improve.

To say that these stories are "essential" means that they have become permanent parts of the literary "canon," and that anyone who is majoring in (or simply interested in) English literature should know a little about them and their authors. And let me also say that knowledge of these stories' characters and their problems—and their struggles to deal with them—has been an "essential" part of my own moral and emotional and intellectual development, and that I hope that the stories will in some way become "essential" to you, too.

Table of Contents

Lesson 1 — **The Tell-Tale Heart** (1843) — 6
Edgar Allan Poe (American)

Lesson 2 — **A Christmas Carol** (1843) — 8
Charles Dickens (British)

Lesson 3 — **The Yellow Wallpaper** (1892) — 10
Charlotte Perkins Gilman (American)

Lesson 4 — **Heart of Darkness** (1899) — 12
Joseph Conrad (Polish-British)

Lesson 5 — **Paul's Case** (1905) — 14
Willa Cather (American)

Lesson 6 — **The Dead** (1914) — 16
James Joyce (Irish)

Lesson 7 — **The Garden Party** (1922) — 18
Katherine Mansfield (New Zealand)

Lesson 8 — **The Rocking-Horse Winner** (1926) — 20
D.H. Lawrence (British)

Lesson 9 — **Hills Like White Elephants** (1927) — 22
Ernest Hemingway (American)

Lesson 10 — **Guests of the Nation** (1931) — 24
Frank O'Connor (Irish)

Lesson 11 — **Roman Fever** (1934) — 26
Edith Wharton (American)

Lesson 12 — **The Use of Force** (1938) — 28
William Carlos Williams (American)

Lesson 13 — **The Girls in Their Summer Dresses** (1939) — 30
Irwin Shaw (American)

Lesson 14 — **The Demon Lover** (1941) — 32
Elizabeth Bowen (Irish)

Lesson 15 — **Goodbye, My Brother** (1951) — 34
John Cheever (American)

Top 30 Essential Short Stories in English: 1843 to 2000
Jim Knudsen

Lesson 16 **The Magic Barrel** (1958) — 36
Bernard Malamud (American)

Lesson 17 **The Ledge** (1959) — 38
Lawrence Sargent Hall (American)

Lesson 18 **Everything That Rises Must Converge** (1961) — 40
Flannery O'Connor (American)

Lesson 19 **A & P** (1961) — 42
John Updike (American)

Lesson 20 **The Invisible Japanese Gentlemen** (1965) — 44
Graham Greene (British)

Lesson 21 **Where Are You Going, Where Have You Been?** (1966) — 46
Joyce Carol Oates (American)

Lesson 22 **The Man to Send Rain Clouds** (1967) — 48
Leslie Marmon Silko (Native American)

Lesson 23 **Are These Actual Miles?** (1972) — 50
Raymond Carver (American)

Lesson 24 **A Loaf of Bread** (1972) — 52
James Alan McPherson (American)

Lesson 25 **The Ones Who Walk Away from Omelas** (1975) — 54
Ursula K. Le Guin (American)

Lesson 26 **Bobby's Room** (1984) — 56
Douglas Dunn (Scottish)

Lesson 27 **The Things They Carried** (1986) — 58
Tim O'Brien (American)

Lesson 28 **The Management of Grief** (1988) — 60
Bharati Mukherjee (Indian-American)

Lesson 29 **The Bear Came Over the Mountain** (1999) — 62
Alice Munro (Canadian)

Lesson 30 **Saboteur** (2000) — 64
Ha Jin (Chinese-American)

Lesson 1

The Tell-Tale Heart (1843)
Edgar Allan Poe (American)

 Reading *Read and listen to this short essay and then do the exercises that follow.*

[1] The adjective "telltale" means revealing, obvious, betraying. In this classic psychological thriller, a man is betrayed by the sound of a beating heart—a telltale sign of his guilt. Guilty of what? Of nothing short of cold-blooded murder!

[2] A good story, Edgar Allen Poe said, should be readable in one sitting and have a **compelling** plot. "The Tell-Tale Heart" more than satisfies both conditions. It is barely ten paragraphs long and breathlessly exciting to read. It is told by an unnamed narrator who tries very hard to **convince** the reader that he is not insane, that he is merely extremely nervous, troubled by an **affliction** that makes him sensitive to ... everything. To prove his sanity, he relates an event from his past. In a nutshell, he committed murder—for the flimsiest of reasons. His nervousness made him do it, he says. "I am NOT crazy!" he insists.

[3] At the time, the narrator lived with an old man who had a "horrible, pale-blue eye." The narrator hates that eye, cannot stand looking at it. So what does he do? One night, he drags the sleeping old man out of bed and suffocates him. But just before he dies, the old man wakes up and lets out a terrified scream.

[4] The narrator chops the body up and buries the remains under the floorboards. Almost immediately, he hears a loud ticking noise. Can it be the old man's beating heart? Then there's a knock on the door. It's the police, **alerted** by a neighbor who heard a scream. The narrator acts cool, at first. The policemen believe the made-up story he tells them. But that beating heart—that terrible ticking noise—gets louder, louder. Surely the police must hear it, too! And then ...

[5] I won't **spoil** it for you. But by all means, read this famous story. The contemporary American writer Joyce Carol Oates calls it a work of genius—"utterly convincing in its pathology, and in its obvious **zest** in its pathology."

Notes betraying 「(秘密などが)漏れている」 cold-blooded 「冷血な」 insane 「正気でない」
cannot stand 「我慢できない」 suffocates 「窒息死させる」 pathology 「病理」

Words in Context

Find the words in bold in the essay that match the definitions/synonyms below. Write the words on the lines.

1. _____ disease; illness; disorder; sickness
2. _____ very interesting; fascinating; enthralling; captivating
3. _____ notified; warned; called attention to
4. _____ ruin; destroy; upset
5. _____ assure; make sure; prove; persuade
6. _____ enthusiasm; zeal; excitement; energy

Reading for Details

Write the requested information about "The Tell-Tale Heart" on the lines. Listen to check your answers.

1. _____ what the narrator insists he is NOT
2. _____ what the narrator hates about the old man
3. _____ how the narrator murders the old man
4. _____ what the old man does just before he dies
5. _____ where the old man's remains are buried
6. _____ what the narrator hears, or thinks he hears
7. _____ who knocks on the door
8. _____ how the narrator acts—at first

Making Conversation

With a partner, complete the conversation below. Listen to check and correct your answers. Then practice the conversation together.

A: How does the essay's author describe "The Tell-Tale Heart"?

B: He calls it a _____.

A: Why can the story be read in one sitting?

B: Because it is _____.

A: What does the author of the essay say the story is like to read?

B: He describes reading it as being _____.

A: What did Joyce Carol Oates have to say about the story?

B: She called it a _____.

Lesson 2

A Christmas Carol (1843)
Charles Dickens (British)

 ▶ **Reading** *Read and listen to this short essay and then do the exercises that follow.*

[1] In English we call someone who is **miserly** and mean a "Scrooge," a word coined from the name of the protagonist of Charles Dickens's "A Christmas Carol," Ebenezer Scrooge. In a way, this long tale is a ghost story. But its ghosts aren't scary, at least not for the reader. But they do frighten Scrooge, the meanest, stingiest misanthrope in all of London. How? By showing him what a **miserable** human being he is—by showing him how he is wasting his life!

[2] It's the holiday season, the happiest time of the year all across England, when love and goodwill are in the air. But not for Scrooge. He **detests** Christmas. "Bah! Humbug!" he says to everyone he meets. But then, at just midnight on Christmas Eve, Scrooge is "haunted" by three spirits. The first, The Ghost of Christmas Past, takes Scrooge back to his unhappy childhood. It shows him how, as a young man, Scrooge destroys a chance for **genuine** happiness and starts to become the bitter, **cruel** man he is today. Next comes the Ghost of Christmas Present, who gives Scrooge a tour of the joys of Christmas—for everyone except Scrooge, that is. And finally comes the Ghost of Christmas Yet to Come, a "draped and hooded" phantom who escorts Scrooge to the cemetery and shows him his lonely, unvisited grave and his own rat-eaten corpse. Inspired by these nighttime "hauntings," Scrooge undergoes a transformation, a change of heart that we can still read today as one that the world sorely needs.

[3] In 1843, Charles Dickens was a wildly popular young novelist. But he was **distressed** by social conditions in England and wanted to create a story that would help bring about real change. So he wrote "A Christmas Carol," in which he offered us his vision of a better world. About the tale, William Thackeray said: "'A Christmas Carol' seems to me a national benefit, and to every man or woman who reads it, a personal kindness."

Notes coined「作られた」 misanthrope「厭世家（人嫌いの人）」
"haunted"「幽霊に悩まされた」 phantom「幽霊」
G.K. Chesterton「イギリスの批評家・作家（1874-1936）」

Words in Context

Find the words in bold in the essay that match the definitions/synonyms below. Write the words on the lines.

1. _____ exceedingly mean; brutal; inhuman; heartless
2. _____ very sad; pathetic; dismal; wretched
3. _____ spending as little money as possible; tightfisted; stingy
4. _____ very concerned or worried; saddened; seriously upset
5. _____ dislikes to the extreme; hates; abhors
6. _____ true; real; authentic

Reading for Details

Write the requested information about "A Christmas Carol" on the lines. Listen to check your answers. T-CD 1-8

1. _____ a word that means the main character in a story
2. _____ what kind of person Ebenezer Scrooge is
3. _____ what's in the air at Christmastime
4. _____ how Scrooge greets the people he meets
5. _____ what kind of childhood Scrooge had
6. _____ the name of the second ghost
7. _____ what that spirit shows Scrooge
8. _____ what Scrooge sees at the cemetery

Making Conversation

With a partner, complete the conversation below. Listen to check and correct your answers. Then practice the conversation together. T-CD 1-9

A: In a way, what kind of story is "A Christmas Carol"?

B: You might say that it is _____.

A: How do the three spirits in the story "frighten" Scrooge?

B: They show him what a _____.

A: In 1843, what was Dickens especially concerned about?

B: He was upset by _____.

A: To whom did William Thackeray say "A Christmas Carol" was a "personal kindness"?

B: It was a personal kindness _____.

Lesson 3

The Yellow Wallpaper (1892)
Charlotte Perkins Gilman (American)

 Reading *Read and listen to this short essay and then do the exercises that follow.*

[1] I've just re-read "The Yellow Wallpaper" and was once again awed by its power—its **innovative** language, fascinating characters, Gothic setting, enduring themes, shocking ending. The story is narrated (in the form of a diary) by an unnamed young bride who suffers from "hysteria"—an old-fashioned word for depression. She has been **diagnosed** by her husband John, a well-meaning though "dominating" physician. He has prescribed a "rest cure" for his wife, a common 19th-century treatment for emotional afflictions of all kinds—especially for women. The narrator is locked up in solitary confinement, with nothing to do except "rest." She **obeys** John because he is her husband, her doctor—and because he is a man.

[2] When the story opens, John has just moved his wife to a large country mansion and put her in an isolated upstairs room with, you guessed it, yellow wallpaper. Here's how the narrator describes it: "A wallpaper whose color is **repellant**, almost revolting, a smoldering unclean yellow … a dull yet lurid orange in some places, a sickly sulphur tint in others." But the room is no cure. Instead, the bored, lonely narrator becomes increasingly **obsessed** with that hated wallpaper, imagining all sorts of "crazy" things about it and what's trapped behind it. And then …

[3] When "The Yellow Wallpaper" came out, most readers saw it as a horror story in the Edgar Allan Poe vein. But that's not what Gilman intended. It was, she admitted, autobiographical: she herself had suffered from "hysteria." She, too, had been **subjected** to a similar "rest cure" that drove her "as far as one could go toward insanity." Gilman meant her story to be a criticism of solitary confinement and of the general condition of women. "Every kind of creature is developed by the exercise of its functions," she once said. "If denied this, the creature cannot develop in the fullest degree."

Notes enduring 「永続的な」   prescribed 「指図する」   lurid 「どぎつい」
functions 「機能」

Words in Context

Find the words in bold in the essay that match the definitions/synonyms below. Write the words on the lines.

1. _____ horrible to see, smell, or touch; disgusting
2. _____ identified an illness by examining signs and symptoms
3. _____ original; fresh; imaginative; inventive
4. _____ always worried or thinking about one thing
5. _____ does what one is told; goes along with; agrees; follows
6. _____ made to experience; forced to undergo

Reading for Details

Write the requested information about "The Yellow Wallpaper" on the lines. Listen to check your answers. 1-13

1. _____ what kind of setting the story has
2. _____ what depression was once called
3. _____ a synonym for "doctor" in paragraph 1
4. _____ a phrase that means "kept all alone in one place"
5. _____ what kind of room the narrator is kept in
6. _____ how the wallpaper's yellow is described
7. _____ what the room is NOT a cure for
8. _____ how most readers saw the story when it came out

Making Conversation

With a partner, complete the conversation below. Listen to check and correct your answers. Then practice the conversation together. 1-14

A: How is "The Yellow Wallpaper" told?

B: It is narrated in the _____.

A: Why does the narrator go along with such a strange cure or treatment?

B: Because her doctor is also _____.

A: Why can the story be said to be "autobiographical"?

B: Because Gilman herself suffered _____.

A: What two things did Gilman see "The Yellow Wallpaper" as a criticism of?

B: She used her story to criticize _____.

Lesson 4

Heart of Darkness (1899)
Joseph Conrad (Polish-British)

Reading *Read and listen to this short essay and then do the exercises that follow.*

[1] Until he was nearly 20, Joseph Conrad (born in Poland in 1857) spoke no English. And yet he went on to become one of the language's greatest prose stylists. Conrad also came to literature **relatively** late in life. He started out as a merchant seaman and eventually worked as a ship's captain before writing his first novel. His best-loved works, like "Heart of Darkness," are mostly set at sea.

[2] The tale is narrated by Marlow, a man who "still follows the sea" but who also enjoys "spinning yarns." Marlow and several friends are relaxing and **reminiscing** on a boat in the Thames River. As dusk falls, Marlow out of the blue says in his typically contemplative way, "The conquest of the earth, which mostly means the taking it away from those who have a different **complexion** or slightly flatter noses than ourselves, is not a pretty thing when you look into it too much."

[3] This denunciation of colonialism leads to Marlow's telling a story about a time when he was a riverboat captain in the Belgian Congo. His mission? To rescue an **enigmatic** European ivory trader named Kurtz who, rumor says, has "gone native" deep in the heart of the darkest jungle. After a long, dangerous journey up the Congo River, Marlow finally reaches Kurtz, who has turned himself into a king of sorts, ruling **tyrannically** over a savage empire. But Kurtz is also deathly ill— and obviously insane. Marlow persuades him to leave and return to Europe with him. And then ...

[4] "Heart of Darkness" is justly admired for its technical skill and powerful descriptions. It has a large cast of complex characters, explores profound ideas, and uses **evocative** symbolism. But the story also has its detractors. One is the Nigerian writer, Chinua Achebe, who described the tale as "offensive and deplorable" and called its author a "thoroughgoing racist." Conrad, says Achebe, "dehumanizes" Africa by showing it as the "antithesis" of European civilization.

Notes contemplative「熟慮した上での」　persuades「説得する」　detractors「誹謗する人」
deplorable「嘆かわしい」　antithesis「正反対（アンチテーゼ）」

Words in Context

Find the words in bold in the essay that match the definitions/synonyms below. Write the words on the lines.

1. _____ mysterious; puzzling
2. _____ causing ideas or images to form in the mind; expressive
3. _____ rather; quite; comparatively
4. _____ thinking and talking about the past; recalling
5. _____ in a cruel and oppressive way; despotically; unjustly
6. _____ skin color

Reading for Details

Write the requested information about "Heart of Darkness" on the lines. Listen to check your answers. *T-CD 1-18*

1. _____ Joseph Conrad's place of birth
2. _____ what Conrad's first career was
3. _____ where and to whom Marlow tells his Congo "yarn"
4. _____ a word in paragraph 3 meaning "harsh criticism"
5. _____ where Marlow's "mission" took place
6. _____ what Kurtz has turned himself into
7. _____ what Marlow persuades Kurtz to do
8. _____ Chinua Achebe's nationality

Making Conversation

With a partner, complete the conversation below. Listen to check and correct your answers. Then practice the conversation together. *T-CD 1-19*

A: What makes Conrad's achievements in English literature so remarkable?
B: He didn't even start learning _____.

A: What does Marlow say about the "conquest of the earth"?
B: He says that it is not a _____.

A: What is "Heart of Darkness" justly admired for?
B: Many people admire it for _____.

A: How does "Heart of Darkness" dehumanize Africa, according to Achebe?
B: It dehumanizes Africa by _____.

Lesson 5

Paul's Case (1905)
Willa Cather (American)

Reading *Read and listen to this short essay and then do the exercises that follow.*

[1]   Willa Cather was a high-school English teacher in Pittsburgh, Pennsylvania, when she wrote "Paul's Case," whose protagonist, Paul, was inspired by two of her students. We've all met "Pauls," young people with a temperament that won't allow them to fit in. Sensitive, romantic, turned off by the world of commerce and materialism, and by everyday life, these "characters" are "defiantly" themselves.

[2]   Some turn to art, and that, vaguely, is what Paul **aspires** to. But for Paul, becoming an artist is unlikely. He has a vivid imagination, for sure, but he lacks the true talent, discipline, and **diligence** that making art requires. What's more, Paul is, in a word, off-putting. He purposely puts himself at odds with everyone he meets. He angers and **perplexes** his father. He has made no close friends at his school—from which he has been suspended for various "misdemeanors" and "disorder and impertinence." Self-centered, snobbish, rude, Paul is a walking self-inflicted wound—his own worst enemy.

[3]   "Until now," Cather tells us, "Paul could not remember the time when he had not been **dreading** something. Even when he was a little boy, it was always there—the shadowed corner, the dark place into which he dared not look, but from which something always seemed to be watching him." So how does Paul avoid this "shadowed corner"? He dreams, he pretends. And he steals $1,000 and runs off to New York City, where he puts himself up at a plush hotel, buys some fancy clothes, and spends a week playing the role of a rich, sophisticated young gentleman. His father comes to take him home and … well, read "Paul's Case" and see.

[4]   Is Willa Cather **condemning** Paul or, worse, **ridiculing** him? Not at all. She later explained that Paul cannot help the "nature" he was born with. His failed "revolt against the homilies by which the world is run" has a certain nobility to it. Cather, like millions of her readers, finds Paul's case both touching and instructive.

Notes   temperament「気性」   turned off「興味を失った」   suspended「停学させられた」
           impertinence「無礼な振る舞い」   homilies「(長々とした)説教」

Words in Context

Find the words in bold in the essay that match the definitions/synonyms below. Write the words on the lines.

1. _____ criticizing very harshly; denouncing; censuring
2. _____ hard work; industriousness; conscientiousness
3. _____ fearing; being afraid of
4. _____ making fun of; mocking
5. _____ hopes or strongly desires to become or do something
6. _____ confuses; baffles

Reading for Details

Write the requested information about "Paul's Case" on the lines. Listen to check your answers. 1-23

1. _____ Willa Cather's other job besides writing fiction
2. _____ a word in paragraph 1 meaning "stubbornly"
3. _____ what Paul lacks for making art
4. _____ what Paul does to his father
5. _____ a word in paragraph 2 that means "minor crimes"
6. _____ how much money Paul steals
7. _____ who Paul "acts" as in New York City
8. _____ a word in paragraph 4 meaning "cliches"

Making Conversation

With a partner, complete the conversation below. Listen to check and correct your answers. Then practice the conversation together. 1-24

A: Who was the inspiration for the protagonist in "Paul's Case"?

B: He was based on _____.

A: What turns off some "sensitive" young people like Paul?

B: They dislike _____.

A: What does the author of the essay imply by "self-inflicted wound"?

B: He implies that Paul causes _____.

A: How does Willa Cather see Paul's "failed revolt" against the system?

B: She believes that there is _____.

Lesson 6

The Dead (1914)
James Joyce (Irish)

Reading *Read and listen to this short essay and then do the exercises that follow.*

[1]   We're in early 20th-century Dublin, Ireland, at a Christmas party hosted by two kind music teachers, the Misses Morkan—a "**splendid** annual affair" that offers guests "the best of everything": refreshment, music, dancing, **convivial** conversation. But there is turmoil in "The Dead," too, mostly in the heart of the central character, Gabriel Conroy. Gabriel is well-meaning, but the problem is, he constantly makes **complacent** assumptions about himself. He believes that he is universally admired and liked, that his comments are always pertinent, his jokes appreciated, his ideas profound. And the speech he will give tonight? It will be the "hit" of the party! But Gabriel's greatest assumptions are about his wife, Gretta.

[2]   At one point during the evening, Gabriel sees Gretta standing motionless at the top of the stairs high above him. She is lost in a **reverie**, with "grace and mystery in her attitude," listening to someone singing an old Irish tune. "Ah, she's thinking of me," Gabriel assumes. He goes even further: He assures himself that her life—its very meaning, the core of her identity—is wrapped up in him.

[3]   Later, in their hotel room, Gabriel makes another assumption: that they will have a night of romantic **bliss**. But no, Gretta is tired and, still, mysteriously lost in thought. "What is it, dear?" Gabriel asks. She then quietly tells him a story that she has kept secret for twenty years. It's about … well, I won't give it away.

[4]   Let's just say that Gretta's story unnerves Gabriel. His assumptions fall away and are replaced by vision. Looking out the window at the falling snow, tears fill his eyes. His sense of self "fades into a grey impalpable world." And in James Joyce's famous final sentence, which the American author Mary Gordon describes as "a **triumph** of pure sound, of language as music," Gabriel sees "the snow falling faintly through the universe and faintly falling, like the descent of their last end, upon all the living and the dead."

Notes pertinent「的を射た」   wrapped up in「〜に夢中になっている」
unnerves「狼狽させる」   impalpable「触っても感じられない」
descent「降りていくこと」

Words in Context

Find the words in bold in the essay that match the definitions/synonyms below. Write the words on the lines.

1. _____ magnificent; grand; wonderful; spectacular
2. _____ victory; huge success; great achievement
3. _____ daydream; meditation; contemplation
4. _____ self-assured; self-satisfied; smug; blithe
5. _____ friendly; companionable; pleasant
6. _____ extreme happiness; ecstasy; elation

Reading for Details

Write the requested information about "The Dead" on the lines. Listen to check your answers.

1. _____ the setting of "The Dead"
2. _____ what the Misses Morkan offer their guests
3. _____ a word in paragraph 1 meaning "disorder; chaos"
4. _____ how Gabriel sees his jokes
5. _____ where Gabriel is when he sees his wife
6. _____ what Gretta is listening to
7. _____ where Gabriel and Gretta spend the night
8. _____ what the weather is like outside the window

Making Conversation

With a partner, complete the conversation below. Listen to check and correct your answers. Then practice the conversation together.

A: What is Gabriel Conroy's biggest problem?

B: The thing is, he tends to _____.

A: What does Gabriel think first when he sees his wife lost in a reverie?

B: He assumes that _____.

A: What happens to many of Gabriel's assumptions at the end of "The Dead"?

B: They _____.

A: In the story's final sentence, on whom does Gabriel see the snow falling?

B: He sees it falling on _____.

Lesson 7

The Garden Party (1922)
Katherine Mansfield (New Zealand)

 1-32 **Reading** *Read and listen to this short essay and then do the exercises that follow.*

[1]   Class conflict is a **perennial** theme of fiction—especially British fiction. "The Garden Party," set among the highbrow classes in early 20th-century New Zealand, confronts this conflict head on. But the story is also a bildungsroman, a coming-of-age tale that chronicles the moral and emotional growth of a sensitive, "artistic," 17-year-old girl named Laura Sheridan.

[2]   The story starts as Laura and her family are getting ready for the big annual party to be held that afternoon on the grounds of their enormous manor house. These hectic preparations go on in full sight and sound of the neighboring ghetto of shabby workingmen's shacks: "The very smoke coming out of their chimneys," writes Mansfield, "was poverty-stricken. Little rags and shreds of smoke, so unlike the great silvery plumes that uncurled from the Sheridans' chimneys."

[3]   Having led a sheltered life, Laura has had little **exposure** to class differences, poverty, death. But these realities are soon forced onto her consciousness by a tragic event: a workingman neighbor has been killed. When news of this accident reaches the Sheridans, Laura is horrified. "We must cancel the party!" she insists. But her sister Jose dismisses Laura's doubts as **absurd**: "Whatever do you mean?" The party must go on, says Laura's mother, the snobbish Mrs. Sheridan, because "such people" don't expect sacrifices from "people like us."

[4]   The party does go on, and Laura, resigned, attends. Afterwards, her mother suggests that she take some leftover party food to the dead man's family. Laura does so and finds them in deep mourning, with the body laid out in one of the rooms. Laura goes in, looks down at the corpse, and …

[5]   Laura's reaction to the scene is **ambiguous**. She seems oddly comforted, even contented. Why? Is she just **elated** to have had a "real" experience, no matter how dark and disturbing—one that her sheltered life has **prohibited**? Has the artist in her finally found "material" to work with? Critics still debate these questions.

Notes   chronicles「年代順に記録する」   hectic「とても忙しい」   sheltered「安全に守られた」

Words in Context

Find the words in bold in the essay that match the definitions/synonyms below. Write the words on the lines.

1. _____ ridiculous; silly; asinine
2. _____ happening all the time; recurring; enduring
3. _____ not allowed or permitted; made impossible; precluded
4. _____ extremely happy or pleased; ecstatic
5. _____ not clear or specifically stated; vague; indistinct
6. _____ a chance to see or experience; knowledge; familiarity

Reading for Details

Write the requested information about "The Garden Party" on the lines. Listen to check your answers.

1. _____ a word that means "upper class"
2. _____ how often the Sheridans' garden party is held
3. _____ where the garden party is held
4. _____ what lies just outside the Sheridans' garden area
5. _____ what kind of life Laura has led until now
6. _____ who Mrs. Sheridan means by "such people"
7. _____ where Laura goes after the party
8. _____ where Laura views the dead man's body

Making Conversation

With a partner, complete the conversation below. Listen to check and correct your answers. Then practice the conversation together.

A: Why can "The Garden Party" be called a bildungsroman?

B: Because it tells of Laura's _____.

A: How is Laura's character described?

B: She is said to be _____.

A: What does the smoke coming from the ghetto's shabby shacks show?

B: It shows how _____.

A: Why might Laura's reaction to the corpse be called unexpected?

B: Because she seems oddly _____.

Lesson

The Rocking-Horse Winner (1926)
D.H. Lawrence (British)

 ▶ **Reading** *Read and listen to this short essay and then do the exercises that follow.*

[1]   Whereas class conflict animates "The Garden Party," it is family **discord** that **permeates** D.H. Lawrence's "The Rocking-Horse Winner." This tension is felt most **acutely** by a young boy named Paul, who discovers that he has a fantastic power that might save his troubled family. Paul, just by rocking his toy rocking-horse, can make money, and lots of it.

[2]   Here are the story's first few lines (the woman is Paul's mother). "There was a woman who was beautiful, who started with all the advantages, yet she had no luck. She married for love, and the love turned to dust. She had bonny children, yet she felt they had been thrust on her, and she could not love them. They looked at her coldly, as if they were finding fault with her. When her children were present, she always felt the centre of her heart go hard."

[3]   What does that language, that style, that tone sound like to you? A fairytale, right—a story for children. It's as if an evil curse has **descended** on the woman and her whole family, as if some cruel witch's spell keeps them frozen in a state of icy misery. Here's another line: "And so the house came to be haunted by the unspoken phrase: There must be more money!"

[4]   That's the evil curse—money, or, more accurately, the want of it. And yet, the family are not poor. They are upper-middle-class and have money, but "not nearly enough for the social position which they had to keep up." Not nearly enough for their extravagance. So, as you can see, the story is not for kids after all. It is rather a **cautionary** tale for grown-ups—a bitter satire on the consumerism and financial obsessions of modern life.

[5]   The depth and beauty of "The Rocking-Horse Winner" cannot be **exaggerated**. But, like "Paul's Case," it's not a feel-good story. As Paul desperately rocks his horse, hoping to make his parents happy, to "win" their love, ... well, read the story and see.

Notes   finding fault with 「あら探しをする」   curse 「罵(ののし)りの言葉」   misery 「惨(みじ)めさ」
extravagance 「浪費」   satire 「風刺」   consumerism 「大量消費主義」

Words in Context

Find the words in bold in the essay that match the definitions/synonyms below. Write the words on the lines.

1. _____ said to be larger or better than in reality
2. _____ lack of harmony; conflict; antagonism
3. _____ sharply; severely; keenly
4. _____ spreads throughout; completely fills
5. _____ serving or acting as a warning; admonishing
6. _____ fell upon as if attacking; invaded; occupied

Reading for Details

Write the requested information about "The Rocking-Horse Winner" on the lines. Listen to check your answers. T-CD 1-38

1. _____ what does the story deal with
2. _____ the story's main consciousness or character
3. _____ what the woman started with but did not have
4. _____ what she felt when she was near her children
5. _____ what the author believes the story sounds like
6. _____ the unspoken phrase that haunts the house
7. _____ what the family tries to "keep up"
8. _____ what Paul hopes to win by rocking his horse

Making Conversation

With a partner, complete the conversation below. Listen to check and correct your answers. Then practice the conversation together. T-CD 1-39

A: What do "The Rocking-Horse Winner" and "Paul's Case" have in common?

B: Neither has _____.

A: What does the essay's author say young Paul's family's unhappiness is like?

B: He says that it is as if _____.

A: Why is the story actually for adults?

B: Because it satirizes _____.

A: What most impresses the essay's author about the story?

B: He is most impressed by its _____.

Lesson 9

Hills Like White Elephants (1927)
Ernest Hemingway (American)

Reading Read and listen to this short essay and then do the exercises that follow.

[1] "Would you please please please please please please please stop talking?" Seven "pleases"—a perfect number rhythmically and thematically—and perfectly in character. This is how an exhausted, **vulnerable** woman named Jig tells the egotistical, bullying man she is with to shut up and leave her alone.

[2] The line comes near the end of "Hills Like White Elephants," a miracle of a short story about a still **contentious** topic: abortion. I say miracle because almost everything in the story—plot, theme, characters, setting—is revealed through Hemingway's typically **subtle**, stylized but absolutely true-to-life dialogue. The word "abortion" isn't spoken. It's just two people **alluding** to "it," but never saying "it" out loud. The word's too ugly, too brutal.

[3] An expatriate American couple—Jig and "the man"—are sitting on a train station platform in Spain, having drinks, waiting, talking. Well, not talking exactly—more like baiting, jabbing at, jousting with each other. Jig looks across the Ebro River. "The hills look like white elephants," she says, hoping to impress the man with her brightness, with her clever simile. But he's not impressed; he has something else on his self-absorbed mind. Jig is pregnant, and he doesn't want the baby, doesn't want the **burden**, the responsibility of fatherhood. He wants freedom, pleasure, power. "It's really an awfully simple operation, Jig," he says, **smugly**, sweetly. "They just let the air in and then it's all perfectly natural. It's the best thing to do. But I don't want you to do it if you don't really want to." Liar!

[4] And what does Jig want? Only to know that if she does go through with "it," that they will be happy again, that their lives will be like before, that he will love her again. Of course, of course, he says. Don't worry. But then he starts up, again: "It's really a perfectly simple operation," he says, on and on. And then Jig just wants to scream. And asks him to please be quiet. Please. Please!

Notes brutal 「残忍な」　baiting 「わなにかける」　jousting 「一騎打ちの戦いをする」
self-absorbed 「自己陶酔の」

Words in Context

Find the words in bold in the essay that match the definitions/synonyms below. Write the words on the lines.

1. _____ a heavy load; responsibility; obligation; duty; worry
2. _____ easily hurt; in danger; at risk; fragile
3. _____ not said openly; delicate; understated
4. _____ in a self-satisfied, superior way; conceitedly; arrogantly
5. _____ controversial; causing debate; disputed
6. _____ suggesting; hinting at; not naming directly

Reading for Details

Write the requested information about "Hills Like White Elephants" on the lines. Listen to check your answers. *T-CD 1-43*

1. _____ a word in paragraph 1 that means "self-centered"
2. _____ how "Hills Like White Elephants" is described
3. _____ how "abortion" is referred to in the story
4. _____ the story's setting
5. _____ how Jig wants to appear to or impress the man
6. _____ a word meaning "expecting a baby"
7. _____ why the man doesn't want the baby
8. _____ what Jig feels like doing towards the end of the story

Making Conversation

With a partner, complete the conversation below. Listen to check and correct your answers. Then practice the conversation together. *T-CD 1-44*

A: Why does Jig say "please" seven times?

B: Probably because she is so tired of _____.

A: What is "typically Hemingway" about the story's dialogue?

B: It is stylized but _____.

A: Instead of just talking, what are Jig and the man doing?

B: They are actually _____.

A: Why does the author of the essay call the man a liar?

B: Because the man _____.

Lesson 10

Guests of the Nation (1931)
Frank O'Connor (Irish)

 Reading Read and listen to this short essay and then do the exercises that follow.

[1]   Frank O'Connor was an **astute** critic of the short story as well as one of its greatest practitioners. He once said, "There is in the short story at its most characteristic something we do not often find in the novel—an intense awareness of human loneliness." The young Irish soldier Bonaparte, who narrates "Guests of the Nation," **exemplifies** what O'Connor meant. At the end of this moving cautionary tale, Bonaparte says, "I was somehow very small and very lost and lonely like a child astray in the snow."

[2]   The story's setting is the Irish War of Independence (1916-1921), when Ireland was fighting to throw off British colonial rule. Two English soldiers, Hawkins and Belcher, stationed in Ireland to help **quell** the Irish rebellion, have been **abducted**. They are being held captive in a rural cottage, and Bonaparte and a fellow Irish Republican Army soldier, Noble, have been ordered to guard them. But over time, the English and Irish "enemies" have become friends. They share histories, play cards, **amiably** argue about religion, culture, and politics. In fact, they are now such good "chums," as Belcher puts it, that Bonaparte no longer sees his charges as prisoners, but as "guests of the nation."

[3]   But then Bonaparte is dismayed to learn that Belcher and Hawkins are not just prisoners of war, not "guests" at all, but hostages who ... well, you'll see. Only know that Bonaparte must perform a "duty" that he is neither mentally nor morally prepared for, one that changes him for good: "Anything that happened to me afterwords," he says, "I never felt the same way about again."

[4]   Re-reading "Guests of the Nation," I was reminded of World War I's "Christmas Truce," when enemy German and British soldiers put down their arms, **emerged** from their trenches, sang Christmas carols together, exchanged gifts, and even enjoyed a friendly game of soccer. But then the cease-fire ended. Reality returned. The soldiers became enemies again, and the war went back to "normal."

Notes colonial rule 「植民地支配」   charges 「託された人々」   hostages 「人質」
trenches 「塹壕」

Words in Context

Find the words in bold in the essay that match the definitions/synonyms below. Write the words on the lines.

1. _____ in a friendly, pleasant way; amicably
2. _____ came out of; appeared
3. _____ put down; suppress; put an end to
4. _____ sharp; clever; intelligent; logical
5. _____ serves as an example of; illustrates; demonstrates
6. _____ captured; taken prisoner; arrested

Reading for Details

Write the requested information about "Guests of the Nation" on the lines. Listen to check your answers. *T-CD 1-48*

1. _____ who Bonaparte is
2. _____ how the author describes "Guests of the Nation"
3. _____ where and when the story is set
4. _____ what Hawkins and Belcher are doing in Ireland
5. _____ where they are being held captive
6. _____ what happens between the guards and "guests"
7. _____ what the guests and "hosts" often do together
8. _____ when the "Christmas Truce" took place

Making Conversation

With a partner, complete the conversation below. Listen to check and correct your answers. Then practice the conversation together. *T-CD 1-49*

A: What does Frank O'Connor say many short stories have as their main theme?

B: Many are about _____.

A: What was the goal of the Irish during the War of Independence?

B: They aimed to _____.

A: What does Bonaparte learn about the "prisoners" that shocks and upsets him?

B: He is told that _____.

A: What is the great irony of the "Christmas Truce"?

B: It is ironic that _____.

Lesson 11

Roman Fever (1934)
Edith Wharton (American)

 ▶ **Reading** *Read and listen to this short essay and then do the exercises that follow.*

[1] The popular American writer O'Henry (real name William Sydney Porter, 1862-1910) is famous for the surprise, ironic endings of his short stories. Sure, they're fun to read, but let's be honest: Many of his "twists" come across as gimmicks. They can be, as the literary critic Susan Lohafer puts it, "simplistic, formulaic, and **trivial**." But, Lohafer adds, the shock ending, when handled by a master, can "jolt us into perceiving something **fundamental** about what we have been reading."

[2] No story better illustrates the "masterful" surprise ending than "Roman Fever." Up until the very last line (which I won't **divulge** here!), you don't know what's coming. It's the early 20th century, and two New York society widows of "ripe middle-age," Mrs. Slade and Mrs. Ansley, are sitting at a terrace cafe on Rome's Janiculum Hill, gazing out at "the best view in the world." They have been friends, off and on, for most of their lives. Having been out of touch recently, they are now enjoying what appears to be a **civil**, catch-up conversation: about their late husbands; about the marriage prospects of their two teenage daughters, who are in Rome with them; about "Roman fever," the malaria that once plagued the Eternal City.

[3] But beneath the politeness and pleasantries lurk envy, jealousy, **hypocrisy**, and resentment. Most of this is reflected in the mind of the **haughty** but ultimately lonely and insecure Mrs. Slade. The talk then turns to a time 25 years earlier, here in Rome, when the two women were teenagers themselves—and rivals for the same man. Suddenly, Mrs. Slade can no longer contain herself. She must have the last say, she thinks, and tells Mrs. Ansley ... well, you'll see. Suffice it to say that all the long-buried bitterness and tension and secrets between the two women come out. And then comes the "jolt" of Edith Wharton's last line, which can make you smile, gasp, nod your head in wonder, all at once. This "twist" is no gimmick.

Notes formulaic「型通りの」   prospects「見込み」   plagued「苦しめた」
"Can no longer contain herself"「もはや抑えきれずに」
"Suffice it to say ..."「あえて言うなら…」

Words in Context

Find the words in bold in the essay that match the definitions/synonyms below. Write the words on the lines.

1. _____ polite; courteous; well-mannered
2. _____ conceited; stuck-up; arrogant
3. _____ of little value or importance; petty; insignificant
4. _____ reveal; tell (a secret); disclose; make public
5. _____ false behavior; pretentiousness; insincerity
6. _____ basic; essential

Reading for Details

Write the requested information about "Roman Fever" on the lines. Listen to check your answers.

1. _____ William Sydney Porter's pseudonym
2. _____ an informal word meaning "trick" or "ploy"
3. _____ who or what Susan Lohafer is
4. _____ where Mrs. Slade and Mrs. Ansley are sitting
5. _____ where their husbands are now
6. _____ who is in Rome with the two women
7. _____ another name for "Roman fever"
8. _____ what the two women were 25 years earlier

Making Conversation

With a partner, complete the conversation below. Listen to check and correct your answers. Then practice the conversation together.

A: What does Susan Lohafer say "good" surprise endings can do?

B: They can jolt us into _____.

A: How are Mrs. Slade and Mrs. Ansley described?

B: They are described as _____.

A: On the surface, what is the two women's conversation like?

B: It _____.

A: What happens when Mrs. Slade tries to have the last say?

B: That's when all the _____.

Lesson 12

The Use of Force (1938)
William Carlos Williams (American)

 ▶ **Reading** *Read and listen to this short essay and then do the exercises that follow.*

[1] We don't usually **associate** the phrase "use of force" with doctors and patients. It almost always applies to law enforcement. Say a peaceful demonstration threatens to turn into a riot, or a hostage crisis shows no signs of ending happily. In such cases, police officers may receive a "use of force" order **authorizing** them to take whatever action they think is needed to resolve the situation.

[2] In "The Use of Force," the phrase describes what should have been a **routine** doctor/patient encounter. A physician, the first-person narrator, is making a house call. A little girl is sick, with a high fever and sore throat. Because diphtheria is going around, the doctor is especially concerned. Using his kindest, most professional bedside manner, he attempts to examine her throat. Perhaps it's just inflamed tonsils—not potentially **fatal** diphtheria after all. But the girl refuses to open her mouth. She is ashamed, terrified. The harder he tries to get her to open up, the more irrational and pig-headed she becomes, "screaming in wild hysterical shrieks" and "clawing **instinctively**" for his eyes. The doctor/narrator finds himself becoming increasingly frustrated, aggressive, and then enraged. "The worst of it was," he says, "I too had got beyond reason. I could have torn the child apart in my own fury and enjoyed it. It was a pleasure to attack her. My face was burning with it."

[3] And then, in "a final unreasoning **assault**, I ..." Well, I won't tell you what the doctor does then. But here's a hint: this very short story's title tells it all. It suggests that "force"—call it violence, power, unreason, the dark side of human nature—always lurks below our humane, civilized surface.

[4] William Carlos Williams was primarily a poet (and a practicing physician, by the way). He knew how to make every word count and was a master of figurative language. Symbolic, metaphorical, ironic, personal—"The Use of Force" is about as close to poetry that prose fiction can get.

Notes
bedside manner 「患者に対する医者の接し方」　　irrational 「理性のない」
pig-headed 「頑固な」　　enraged 「激怒した」　　humane 「人間味」

Words in Context

Find the words in bold in the essay that match the definitions/synonyms below. Write the words on the lines.

1. _____ deadly; causing death
2. _____ normal; everyday; usual; average
3. _____ allowing or giving permission; approving; consenting
4. _____ attack; aggression
5. _____ in a natural, innate, intuitive way
6. _____ connect or relate in the mind or imagination; equate

Reading for Details

Write the requested information about "The Use of Force" on the lines. Listen to check your answers. T+CD 2-7

1. _____ a phrase that means "the job of a policeman"
2. _____ a crowd of angry people who are causing trouble
3. _____ what kind of situation "The Use of Force" is about
4. _____ why the doctor is especially worried about the girl
5. _____ why the doctor wants to examine the girl's throat
6. _____ how the girl screams
7. _____ what the doctor's face was "burning" with
8. _____ William Carlos Williams's "side job"

Making Conversation

With a partner, complete the conversation below. Listen to check and correct your answers. Then practice the conversation together. T+CD 2-8

A: What does a "use of force" order allow police officers to do?

B: It authorizes them to take whatever _____.

A: At first, how does the doctor/narrator try to get a look at the girl's throat?

B: He uses _____.

A: What are some synonyms for "force" that the essay's author suggests?

B: He calls it _____.

A: Why was William Carlos Williams able to make the story so "close to poetry"?

B: Because he was a poet who could _____.

Lesson 13

The Girls in Their Summer Dresses (1939)
Irwin Shaw (American)

 Reading *Read and listen to this short essay and then do the exercises that follow.*

[1]   In a 1984 interview, Irwin Shaw, author of many novels and short-story collections, tried to shore up his fading reputation: "Back in the 30s and 40s I was a cult figure ... Now I'm considered just a popular writer. But I think I'm writing more tightly now, with more wisdom, less **vanity**. Now I have peripheral vision."

[2]   As a "cult figure," Shaw had been admired by critics for his **adept** plotting, precise language, and strong characters. But after he wrote and published a string of "popular" novels, his literary stature **waned**, and today, his longer works aren't much read. But several of his short stories remain "classics," **scrupulously** studied in college creative-writing courses, particularly for their masterful dialogue.

[3]   My favorite of these stories is the satirical "The Girls in Their Summer Dresses." A young couple "with money to throw away" are walking along New York City's Fifth Avenue, enjoying an unseasonably warm November Sunday. As they cross Eighth Street, the wife, Frances, says good-naturedly, half-jokingly, "Look out! You'll break your neck!" She has caught her husband Michael ogling a beautiful woman in a revealing summer dress. They laugh it off, keep walking, keep talking, happy to have the whole day to spend together, just the two of them.

[4]   But then Michael does "it" again. This time, though, it's **blatant**, and Frances isn't amused; she's fed up: "I could have a fine Sunday if you didn't look as though you were dying to run after every skirt on Fifth Avenue." Michael denies, protests, swears that he "has not touched another woman. Not once. In all the five years." But Frances isn't buying it. The talk turns hurtful, wicked. And then ...

[5]   Other less skillful authors might have just told us what we need to know about Michael and Frances—her shallowness and neediness, his mediocrity and immature carelessness. But Shaw lets us listen in and then makes us cringe as they tear into each other and show us—all by themselves—how **doomed** they are.

Notes
peripheral「周辺の」 good-naturedly「愛想よく」 ogling「いやらしく見つめる」
fed up「うんざりする」 wicked「ひどく悪い」 mediocrity「平凡さ」

The Girls in Their Summer Dresses ❖ Irwin Shaw

▶ Words in Context
Find the words in bold in the essay that match the definitions/synonyms below. Write the words on the lines.

1. _____ very carefully; meticulously; thoroughly
2. _____ done in an open, unashamed way; obvious; undisguised
3. _____ too much pride in one's appearance or achievements
4. _____ began to decrease; faded; lost power or influence
5. _____ headed or destined for destruction; fated to disaster
6. _____ skillful; expert; consummate; highly proficient

▶ Reading for Details
Write the requested information about "The Girls in Their Summer Dresses" on the lines. Listen to check your answers. *T-CD 2-12*

1. _____ when Shaw was a "cult" figure
2. _____ what critics once admired Shaw for
3. _____ Shaw's works that are not much read today
4. _____ what "with money to throw away" implies
5. _____ the story's setting
6. _____ how Frances feels the next time Michael does "it"
7. _____ what Michael swears he hasn't done
8. _____ a word in paragraph 5 meaning "to feel suddenly awkward, embarrassed, and uncomfortable"

▶ Making Conversation
With a partner, complete the conversation below. Listen to check and correct your answers. Then practice the conversation together. *T-CD 2-13*

A: In 1984, how did Irwin Shaw try to defend his fading reputation?

B: He did it by saying that he _____.

A: Why are Shaw's stories still studied in creative-writing courses?

B: They are still studied mostly _____.

A: What does Frances imply by saying, "You'll break your neck"?

B: She is humorously hinting that Michael is _____.

A: Why most likely does the author say that Michael and Frances are "doomed"?

B: He probably means that they will always _____.

31

Lesson 14

The Demon Lover (1941)
Elizabeth Bowen (Irish)

 Reading *Read and listen to this short essay and then do the exercises that follow.*

[1] The two great **cataclysmic** events of the 20th century, World Wars I and II, are unforgettably linked through Mrs. Drover, the protagonist of Elizabeth Bowen's **eerie** 1941 story, "The Demon Lover." The Blitz—the nighttime attacks on London by German Nazi bombers in 1940 and 1941—has forced Mrs. Drover and her family to flee to the countryside. But on this humid August day, Mrs. Drover has returned for a brief visit to her shut-up London home on a leafy Kensington street, which has become "an unused channel" where "an unfamiliar queerness had silted up."

[2] But that's not all that's "queer." Stepping inside her empty house, Mrs. Drover finds a mysterious letter on the hall table. How did it get there? Who could it be from? At first, she is reluctant to read it, but then curiosity gets the best of her. She opens and reads the brief message, evidently from a former fiancé. Today, the letter reminds her, is the anniversary of the day 25 years earlier, during World War I, when he was leaving to fight on the front in France—the same day Mrs. Drover **solemnly** promised to wait for him. Now, the letter says, it's time for them to meet "at the hour arranged."

[3] What? How? Impossible! The man had soon been reported missing and **presumed** dead. Mrs. Drover had eventually married, had children and became the "keystone of her family life." Perplexed and terrified, she runs out to catch a taxi to take her to the train station. And then …

[4] If ambiguity is a necessary **trait** of modern literature, then "The Demon Lover" is thoroughly modern. What does it all mean? Is it "just" a suspenseful tale of the supernatural? Has the fiancé somehow survived and come back to force Mrs. Drover to honor her promise? Is she being "haunted" by guilt? Or is it all a **hallucination**, a confusing of fantasy and reality in Mrs. Drover's mind, the consequence of the strain and exhaustion of living daily with war—of living under the constant threat of violence and death?

Notes humid「湿気の多い」 gets the best of「〜を負かす」 honor「守る」
strain「精神的な緊張」

Words in Context

Find the words in bold in the essay that match the definitions/synonyms below. Write the words on the lines.

1. _____ disastrous; catastrophic; calamitous; tragic
2. _____ characteristic; feature; aspect
3. _____ odd; strange; uncanny; weird; freakish; ghostly
4. _____ thought or believed to be; assumed; supposed; surmised
5. _____ something seen but not really there; dream; delusion
6. _____ earnestly; seriously; gravely

Reading for Details

Write the requested information about "The Demon Lover" on the lines. Listen to check your answers. T-CD 2-17

1. _____ at what time of day the Blitz bombings occurred
2. _____ where Mrs. Drover and her family have escaped to
3. _____ where Mrs. Drover finds the mysterious letter
4. _____ who appears to have written the letter
5. _____ 25 years ago, where her fiancé was going
6. _____ when the letter says the two should meet
7. _____ the condition of having many possible meanings
8. _____ the kind of tale "The Demon Lover" might "just" be

Making Conversation

With a partner, complete the conversation below. Listen to check and correct your answers. Then practice the conversation together. T-CD 2-18

A: How are World War I and World War II linked in "The Demon Lover"?

B: They are _____.

A: What is implied by the Kensington street's having become "an unused channel"?

B: I think the author implies that _____.

A: Why can "The Demon Lover" be considered "thoroughly modern"?

B: Because it's not clear _____.

A: What might have caused Mrs. Drover to be "hallucinating"?

B: Perhaps it's because living with war has _____.

Lesson 15

Goodbye, My Brother (1951)
John Cheever (American)

 Reading *Read and listen to this short essay and then do the exercises that follow.*

[1]   We all know them: sad, gloomy people who always ruin our good time and darken our mood by finding something, anything, to complain about, criticize, and **ridicule**. We've met them at work, at school, and—perhaps—in our own family, which is what happens and becomes the source of conflict in John Cheever's "Goodbye, My Brother."

[2]   The Pommeroys are an old American family who, "despite their differences," have remained "close in spirit" and loyal to one another. "Any rupture in this loyalty is a source of confusion and pain," says the older-brother narrator. The four Pommeroy children, now middle-aged, have gotten together with their widowed mother for the annual family reunion and two-week holiday. They are relaxing and enjoying themselves at their summer home on an island off the coast of Massachusetts. Lawrence, the youngest sibling—the family member with whom the others have the least in common—hasn't joined them in years. But now he telephones to say that he and his family are on their way.

[3]   Everyone is pleased, but also **wary**: Lawrence is difficult, hypercritical, **morose**—and so are his wife and children. Characteristically, the moment he arrives, he starts complaining: the house is beyond repair and sinking into the sea; the sister, Diana, is cheap and promiscuous; the mother is a lush. And the narrator? "You're a fool," Lawrence tells him. Predictably, Lawrence's gloominess creates an uneasy tension that eventually leads the **exasperated** narrator to ask, "Oh, what can you do with a man like that? How can you teach him to respond to the inestimable greatness of the race, the harsh surface beauty of life?"

[4]   Lawrence, Cheever implies, is a remnant of the old New England Puritan Christian ethic that says that people are sinful and weak, that life is a struggle against painful realities. **Austerity**, hard labor, and repentance are people's destiny and duty. "Goodbye, My Brother" **refutes** that idea. In its glorious ending, in its optimism and beautiful prose, the story rejects Lawrence's dark vision and urges us to get as much joy out of life as we can.

Notes   rupture「不和」   widowed「未亡人」   hypercritical「人を酷評する」
lush = alcoholic「大酒飲み」   inestimable「計り知れない」

Goodbye, My Brother ❖ *John Cheever*

Words in Context

Find the words in bold in the essay that match the definitions/synonyms below. Write the words on the lines.

1. _____ cautious; careful; concerned
2. _____ very frustrated; irritated
3. _____ says no to; proves wrong or incorrect; disagrees with
4. _____ make fun of; laugh at; deride; make a mockery of
5. _____ dark; gloomy; depressed; sad; cranky
6. _____ denial of pleasure and luxury; frugality; abstemiousness

Reading for Details

Write the requested information about "Goodbye, My Brother" on the lines. Listen to check your answers. T•CD 2-22

1. _____ what sad, gloomy people can often ruin
2. _____ who the Pommeroys are
3. _____ how old the Pommeroy children are now
4. _____ where their summer home is located
5. _____ what Lawrence hasn't done recently
6. _____ what Lawrence says is happening to the house
7. _____ what Lawrence calls the mother and the narrator
8. _____ a word in paragraph 4 that means "leftover"

Making Conversation

With a partner, complete the conversation below. Listen to check and correct your answers. Then practice the conversation together. T•CD 2-23

A: What causes the conflict in "Goodbye, My Brother"?

B: Trouble comes because one family member is _____.

A: What can cause confusion and pain among the Pommeroys?

B: This happens when there is any _____.

A: What does the story's narrator wish Lawrence could better appreciate?

B: He is sad that Lawrence doesn't respond to _____.

A: What does the old Puritan Christian ethic have to say about people?

B: That old way of thinking says that _____.

Lesson 16

The Magic Barrel (1958)
Bernard Malamud (American)

 Reading *Read and listen to this short essay and then do the exercises that follow.*

[1]   Saul Bellow, Philip Roth, I.B. Singer—these are the great modern Jewish-American writers. Their often tragicomic stories of immigrants from Europe struggling to "fit in" in the New World **energized** post-war American literature. One more master belongs on that list: Bernard Malamud, author of "The Magic Barrel."

[2]   To summarize the story: For six years, Leo Finkle, a 27-year-old scholar, has **immersed** himself in the study of Jewish religious law. Soon to become a rabbi, he is told that he needs a wife "to attract a congregation." But being socially inept, and having had no time for "the company of women," Leo decides to hire a marriage broker, Pinye Salzman. Salzman calls on Leo in his **meager** New York flat and shows Leo a "thin packet of much-handled cards" with the names and particulars (age, family, education, dowry) of six marriage prospects. Leo arrogantly rejects them all—Too old! Too unattractive! No widows!—and **abruptly** dismisses the matchmaker.

[3]   But the next day, Salzman reappears. Through his "creative salesmanship," he persuades Leo to "try" a woman named Lily, who turns out to be much older than Salzman has led Leo to believe. But, Leo realizes, Salzman has lied to Lily about him, too. He has made Leo out to be a **devout** "Wonder Rabbi," which, Leo confesses to Lily, is far from the truth. This self-realization raises doubts in Leo's mind about his faith and future as a rabbi, and he becomes deeply depressed. Months later, Salzman reappears, this time with photographs of **eligible** girls. Leo turns his nose up at them all. But then one photo …

[4]   I could talk on and on about the story's themes of alienation and salvation, its religious symbolism, its literary roots in folklore and "magical realism," its social commentary. But what I love most about the story is Salzman. His enthusiasm for his matchmaking mission, his idiosyncratic English, his jokes, and his mysteriously "angelic" comings and goings make him and "The Magic Barrel" a reader's delight.

Notes   dowry「花嫁の持参金」   dismisses「解雇する」   idiosyncratic「独特な」

Words in Context

Find the words in bold in the essay that match the definitions/synonyms below. Write the words on the lines.

1. _____ small and insignificant; of bad quality; paltry; bare; slight
2. _____ desirable as a marriage partner; available; suitable
3. _____ deeply involved or absorbed in; occupied; engaged
4. _____ deeply religious; pious; God-loving
5. _____ inspired; invigorated; boosted
6. _____ all of a sudden; just like that; rudely; curtly; sharply

Reading for Details

Write the requested information about "The Magic Barrel" on the lines. Listen to check your answers. T-CD 2-27

1. _____ three great post-war Jewish-American writers
2. _____ Leo Finkle's age and occupation
3. _____ a word meaning "synagogue audience"
4. _____ what Leo has not had time for
5. _____ the "particulars" on Salzman's cards
6. _____ what Salzman told Lily that Leo was
7. _____ what Leo does with Salzman's photographs, at first
8. _____ a word meaning "a feeling of loneliness and isolation"

Making Conversation

With a partner, complete the conversation below. Listen to check and correct your answers. Then practice the conversation together. T-CD 2-28

A: What do the heroes of the stories of Jewish-American writers struggle to do?

B: They have a hard time _____.

A: What reasons does Leo give for rejecting Salzman's marriage prospects?

B: He says that they are _____.

A: What kind of stories does "The Magic Barrel" resemble?

B: It has roots in _____.

A: What are some things about Salzman that impress the author of the essay?

B: He loves Salzman's _____.

Lesson 17

The Ledge (1959)
Lawrence Sargent Hall (American)

 Reading *Read and listen to this short essay and then do the exercises that follow.*

[1] "The Ledge" is set on the Maine coast on Christmas Day. A man—unnamed but described as "big, raw with too much strength" and "incurably male"—arises before sunup. He has promised to take his adolescent son and nephew duck hunting. His wife pleads with him not to go. But he is **adamant**: he's a man who keeps his word! And he wants the boys to experience "a man's sport." Besides, it's a perfect day for duck hunting. So the three of them set out in their boat for a small rocky ledge called Devil's Hump. The man has **fastidiously** planned everything. They will arrive at the ledge just when the tide has **receded** enough to allow them a few hours of good shooting. But then …

[2] "The Ledge," which I first read in a high-school English class, was the story that got me "hooked" on reading. I was new to "good" writing and had some naive but also "snobbish" **notions** about literature. As I read I remember thinking to myself, "No plot or conflict. People too 'common.' Language too simple. Can this be 'real' literature?"

[3] But then came the story's ending. I **gasped** and went straight back to the beginning. How had Hall done it? How had he made something so gut-wrenching and heart-rending—so beautiful—out of such "common" material? I re-read "The Ledge" right away, and learned something very basic: great fiction all boils down to character. The man—his "character"—*is* the plot. He *is* the conflict. What happens happens because of the kind of man he is. He's only "common" in that he is universal.

[4] "The Ledge" is a "textbook" example of what makes short stories so satisfying. Many writers and critics consider it one of the greatest stories ever written, including John Updike, who said in his introduction to *The Best American Short Stories of the Century*: "'The Ledge' is timeless—a naturalistic **anecdote** terrible in its tidal simplicity and inexorability, fatally weighted in every detail."

Notes
gut-wrenching 「はらわたが抉られるような」 heart-rending 「胸が張り裂けるような」
inexorability 「容赦のなさ」

Words in Context
Find the words in bold in the essay that match the definitions/synonyms below. Write the words on the lines.

1. _____ took a quick, deep breath; caught one's breath
2. _____ ideas; beliefs; feelings; impressions; hunches
3. _____ refusing to change one's mind; determined; stubborn
4. _____ a short, interesting, often personal story
5. _____ moved back; retreated; withdrew; ebbed
6. _____ very carefully; meticulously; scrupulously

Reading for Details
Write the requested information about "The Ledge" on the lines. Listen to check your answers. *T-CD 2-32*

1. _____ the setting of "The Ledge"
2. _____ a word meaning "never getting better"
3. _____ what kind of day the man thinks it is
4. _____ what Devil's Hump is
5. _____ how the man and the boys get to Devil's Hump
6. _____ where the author first read the story
7. _____ as he read, what he thought about the characters
8. _____ what "The Ledge" is a "textbook" example of

Making Conversation
With a partner, complete the conversation below. Listen to check and correct your answers. Then practice the conversation together. *T-CD 2-33*

A: Why does the man want to take the boys duck hunting?
B: Because he wants them _____.
A: What time will they arrive at Devil's Hump?
B: They will get there _____.
A: How does the author of the essay describe his old ideas about literature?
B: He says that they _____.
A: What basic thing did the author learn from re-reading "The Ledge"?
B: He learned that _____.

Lesson 18

Everything That Rises Must Converge (1961)

Flannery O'Connor (American)

©GettyImages

 ▶ **Reading** *Read and listen to this short essay and then do the exercises that follow.*

[1] "Everything That Rises Must **Converge**" is set in America's Deep South during the early years of the civil rights era. It was a time when African Americans were struggling for the right to enter "For Whites Only" public places and transportation—when they were fighting for their basic human rights and freedoms.

[2] Here's the story's first sentence: "Her doctor had told Julian's mother that she must lose twenty pounds on account of her blood pressure, so on Wednesday nights Julian had to take her downtown on the bus for a reducing class at the Y." Julian, the story's main character, "had to take her" because his mother, proud of her white **ancestry**, nostalgic for the "good old days" of segregation, distrustful of and repulsed by "Negroes," is a racist and afraid to ride on the newly integrated buses at night. Julian, however, is a recent college graduate and likes to see himself as **enlightened** about race and social change. But the trouble is, Julian's also a bit of a prig, with a cruel streak, to boot.

[3] Julian is always looking for a chance to teach his mother a lesson—to shame her out of her **bigoted** ways. As they get ready to leave one Wednesday, she puts on a new hat that Julian finds "**hideous** and pathetic." But he tells her it looks fine because he gets a **perverse** pleasure out of thinking how ridiculous it will make her look. They get on the bus, sit down. But then a black woman gets on and sits across from them. Incredibly, she is wearing the exact same hat as Julian's mother! "Julian could not believe that Fate had thrust upon his mother such a lesson." And then …

[4] Yes, "Everything That Rises Must Converge" is about race. But it's also about how petty pride and arrogance keep us from truly connecting (converging) with others. In the end, it's Julian who learns the lesson, and it's a harsh one. Here's the story's final line: "The tide of darkness seemed to sweep him back to [his mother], postponing from moment to moment his entry into the world of guilt and sorrow."

Notes struggling 「もがいている」 segregation 「人種差別」 repulsed 「嫌悪感を抱く」
cruel streak 「非情な性格」 sorrow 「後悔」

Everything That Rises Must Converge ❖ Flannery O'Connor

▶ Words in Context

Find the words in bold in the essay that match the definitions/synonyms below. Write the words on the lines.

1. _____ prejudiced; discriminatory; racist
2. _____ behaving in an unexpected, unacceptable way; contrary
3. _____ come together; unite; join; merge; connect; link up
4. _____ forebears; predecessors; heritage; ethnic origins
5. _____ knowledgeable and understanding; broad-minded
6. _____ very ugly; grotesque; repellent; unsightly

▶ Reading for Details

Write the requested information about "Everything That Rises Must Converge" on the lines. Listen to check your answers. 🎧 *2-37*

1. _____ where and when the story is set
2. _____ Julian's mother's health problem
3. _____ how the mother feels about "Negroes"
4. _____ what has happened to Julian recently
5. _____ a word that means "an arrogant, smug person"
6. _____ how Julian thinks the hat makes his mother look
7. _____ who gets on the bus after Julian and his mother
8. _____ what is incredible about the other passenger

▶ Making Conversation

With a partner, complete the conversation below. Listen to check and correct your answers. Then practice the conversation together. 🎧 *2-38*

A: For whom had public places in the South previously been reserved?

B: They had _____.

A: Why can Julian's mother be called a racist?

B: Basically because she is nostalgic _____.

A: What essentially does Julian hope will happen to his mother?

B: He hopes that she will be _____.

A: What does the last line of the story say about Julian's future?

B: It says that he is about to _____.

41

Lesson 19

A & P (1961)
John Updike (American)

 Reading *Read and listen to this short essay and then do the exercises that follow.*

[1]   A&P was once the largest supermarket chain in the U.S., with stores in nearly every town and neighborhood. Its logo—a red circle with thick, white capital letters—was as familiar as the Walmart logo is today. John Updike's contemporary classic story, "A&P," is set in an A&P store in the late 1950s, during the chain's **heyday**.

[2]   I like "loss of innocence" stories in which the protagonist, **typically** a teenager or young adult, recognizes, through an eye-opening experience, how cruel and unpredictable and unfair life can be. Ernest Hemingway's story "The Killers" is one of the most frequently cited examples. Nick Adams, the young person, learns that a man he knows and likes is about to be assassinated by two gangster "killers" who have come into the diner where Nick works. In the end, all the newly awakened and disillusioned Nick can say is, "It's too damned awful."

[3]   The protagonist of "A&P" (a teenager named Sammy) has a similar **epiphany**, though Sammy's "awakening" has nothing to do with violence. The story (narrated in an **endearing** vernacular by Sammy himself) is simple: Sammy is clerking at an A&P when, as he tells us, "In walks these three girls in nothing but bathing suits." Grocery shopping in swim suits! Not proper! At least not back in those stricter, stuffier days. Sammy is naturally attracted to the girls (who are his age) but also envies them their **brazen** lack of concern for social norms and what others think. But the store's prudish older manager, Lengel, is shocked. He scolds and humiliates the girls in front of the other customers (who are also offended by the girls' "indecent dress"). This heartless show of power, of class **condescension**, of injustice angers Sammy who … well, let's not spoil it.

[4]   Just know that Sammy's loss of innocence comes not only because he now sees the world more realistically. It also comes because he senses that his new-found knowledge about life and his own character means that from now on he is going to have a very difficult time "fitting in."

Notes   **vernacular**「方言」   **norms**「規範」   **prudish**「上品ぶった」

A & P ◆ *John Updike*

▶ Words in Context

Find the words in bold in the essay that match the definitions/synonyms below. Write the words on the lines.

1. _____ causing or inspiring affection and love; appealing
2. _____ a time or era of greatest activity or success
3. _____ a snobbish way of behaving, thinking, or speaking
4. _____ shameless; bold; not caring how others see you
5. _____ a sudden realization that changes and inspires you
6. _____ usually; characteristically; ordinarily

▶ Reading for Details

Write the requested information about "A & P" on the lines. Listen to check your answers. *T-CD 2-42*

1. _____ what type of business A&P was
2. _____ typical protagonists of "loss of innocence" stories
3. _____ a word that a means "murdered"
4. _____ Sammy's job at A&P
5. _____ what in those days was not proper in a store
6. _____ how Lengel the store manager is described
7. _____ what offends the other customers in the store
8. _____ how Sammy sees Lengel's show of power

▶ Making Conversation

With a partner, complete the conversation below. Listen to check and correct your answers. Then practice the conversation together. *T-CD 2-43*

A: What does the protagonist of a "loss of innocence" story come to realize?

B: He or she comes to see how _____.

A: What does Nick Adams think is "too damned awful"?

B: He thinks it's awful that _____.

A: How are Nick's and Sammy's epiphanies different?

B: Sammy's awakening _____.

A: What does Sammy learn from the experience in the A&P store?

B: He now sees _____.

Lesson 20

The Invisible Japanese Gentlemen (1965)
Graham Greene (British)

 Reading *Read and listen to this short essay and then do the exercises that follow.*

[1]   The narrator of this very short story is a "literary" author dining at Bentley's, a fashionable seafood restaurant in Mayfair, London's most **affluent** neighborhood. Sitting nearby are eight Japanese gentlemen. Between them and the narrator are a young couple whose accent identifies them as "upper class." The girl (around twenty, very pretty) has just sold the rights to her first novel. Very pleased with herself, she wants to get married—right away. Money won't be an issue, she says. She has received a **substantial** advance, and her editor assures her that her great powers of observation promise a bright future. The young man is not so sure. "Better to wait and see," he says. They leave the restaurant, still talking, still undecided.

[2]   The first time I read "The Invisible Japanese Gentlemen," thirty years ago, I thought the girl silly, spoiled, bossy, **risible**—which is exactly how the narrator wants us to see her. Her "hard commercial attitude" **dismays** him. She lacks, he says, the endurance to "make it" as a real writer. And the narrator pities the young man, who, he says, is "doomed to defeat." Exactly, I thought back then.

[3]   But now, after re-reading the story—after all that has happened socially, historically, and personally since that first time—I don't quite trust the narrator. His comments seem cynical, prudish, sexist, overly proud and defensive of his art. His description of the Japanese men comes across as offensively stereotypical. The young man, seemingly sensible and **pragmatic** on first reading, now appears as wary, **timid**, unadventurous—already an "old man."

[4]   And the girl? I like her. I admire her confidence, ambition, optimism, courage, and desire for independence. After all, she *has* written a novel and already has plans for another—and she's only twenty! As for her "powers of observation," which the narrator so smugly satirizes ... well, who cares if the Japanese gentlemen are "invisible" to her? She's just too focused on hope and love and her bright future to notice. And the young man? He's lucky to have her!

Notes rights「版権」 won't be an issue「問題でない」 pities「哀れむ」
wary「用心深い」 timid「気が小さい」 smugly「気取って」

The Invisible Japanese Gentlemen ✦ *Graham Greene*

▶ Words in Context

Find the words in bold in the essay that match the definitions/synonyms below. Write the words on the lines.

1. _____ sensible; practical; having common sense; prudent
2. _____ saddens or disappoints; distresses
3. _____ wealthy; well-off; prosperous
4. _____ large in amount; significant; considerable; sizable
5. _____ shy; bashful; nervous; diffident
6. _____ causing laughter; comical

▶ Reading for Details

Write the requested information about "The Invisible Japanese Gentlemen" on the lines. Listen to check your answers.   T-CD 2-47

1. _____ what kind of author the narrator of the story is
2. _____ how Bentley's is described
3. _____ what promises the girl a bright future
4. _____ when the essay's author first read the story
5. _____ a word that means "the ability to keep going"
6. _____ what the narrator predicts for the young man
7. _____ what the story's narrator is so eager to defend
8. _____ why the young man already seems "old"

▶ Making Conversation

With a partner, complete the conversation below. Listen to check and correct your answers. Then practice the conversation together.   T-CD 2-48

A: How can readers of the story know that the young couple are "upper class"?

B: We can tell _____.

A: What has affected the essay author's opinion of the story?

B: Since his first reading, a lot _____.

A: Now, how does the author see the narrator's picture of the Japanese?

B: He calls it _____.

A: Now, how does the author feel about the young woman?

B: He is impressed by her _____.

Lesson 21

Where Are You Going, Where Have You Been? (1966)
Joyce Carol Oates (American)

©Larry D. Moor

 Reading *Read and listen to this short essay and then do the exercises that follow.*

[1] This is not a pleasant story. In fact, it's downright creepy. There's a "bad guy" in it who is as **malevolent** as they come. And yet it is one of my favorites. But not just mine. Since it first appeared, it has been required reading in many university English courses. It has also been controversial, with critics and graduate students disputing and "deconstructing" it, looking for hidden meanings, sources, symbols, and allusions, all of which when you hear them sound quite **plausible**.

[2] Oates herself says she based the story on a magazine article about an Arizona serial killer named Charles Schmid, who used music to **lure** his teenage victims, earning him the epithet "The Pied Piper of Tucson." His crimes also earned him a for-life prison sentence (which ended in 1975 when he was stabbed to death by fellow inmates).

[3] "Where Are You Going, Where Have You Been?" is set in mid-60s America, a time of great social **turmoil**, when conventional values, sexual **mores**, and old beliefs were being challenged and rejected. This confusion is reflected in Connie, the pretty fifteen-year-old protagonist. "Everything about her had two sides to it," the omniscient narrator tells us, "one for home and one for anywhere that was not home." One summer evening, Connie goes to a drive-in restaurant with some friends. At a moment when "She drew her shoulders up and sucked in her breath with the pure pleasure of being alive"—when she was at her most **alluring**—she is spotted by a "boy with shaggy black hair" who says to her, "Gonna get you, baby." The next day, the boy mysteriously shows up at Connie's house. And then ... well, you'll see.

[4] I've read this story many times trying to figure out what it "really" means. Oates has written that her story is essentially about a "shallow, vain, silly, hopeful, doomed young girl ... who is capable of an unexpected gesture of heroism at the story's end." That sounds about right.

Notes deconstructing「脱構築」   allusions「言及」

Where Have You Been, Where Are You Going? ✧ Joyce Carol Oates

Words in Context

Find the words in bold in the essay that match the definitions/synonyms below. Write the words on the lines.

1. _____ believable; credible; possible
2. _____ chaos; upheaval; momentous change
3. _____ evil; devilish; demonic; wicked
4. _____ attractive; tempting
5. _____ tempt or attract
6. _____ the traditions or customs of a culture or community

Reading for Details

Write the requested information about "Where Are You Going, Where Have You Been?" on the lines. Listen to check your answers.

1. _____ an informal word that means weird or disturbing
2. _____ where this story is often taught
3. _____ what kind of criminal Charles Schmid was
4. _____ how old Connie was in the mid-60s
5. _____ where Connie goes one evening, and with whom
6. _____ who "spotted" Connie there
7. _____ how Connie's story is told
8. _____ how Oates once described Connie

Making Conversation

With a partner, complete the conversation below. Listen to check and correct your answers. Then practice the conversation together.

A: What do critics like to look for in the story?

B: They hope to find _____.

A: How did Charles Schmid earn his epithet, "The Pied Piper of Tucson"?

B: He was called that because he _____.

A: What are Connie's "two sides"?

B: One side is for _____.

A: What does Connie do at the end of the story, according to Oates?

B: Oates says Connie performs _____.

Lesson 22

The Man to Send Rain Clouds (1967)
Leslie Marmon Silko (Native American)

©GettyImages

▶ **Reading** *Read and listen to this short essay and then do the exercises that follow.*

[1]   To appreciate this masterpiece, you should know that Leslie Marmon Silko is of Native-American, Mexican-American, and Anglo-American ancestry; that the story takes place on the Laguna Reservation of the Pueblo Tribe of Native Americans in New Mexico; and that after the white man invaded the New World in the 1500s, he brutally, **remorselessly** stole the land from the **indigenous** people. Most surviving Native Americans were forced to live in areas called "reservations," where, **ostensibly**, they could preserve their native lifestyles and practice their traditional customs and religions. One more thing: life on the reservations was (and often still is) as impoverished as that in some Third-World countries.

[2]   Here's the story. A man and his brother-in-law find their old grandfather, Teofilo, lying dead beside a cottonwood tree near where Teofilo tended sheep. They tie a gray feather in his long white hair and dab white, blue, yellow, and green paint onto his face, preparing him for the afterlife. "Bring us rain clouds, Grandfather," they say, because in the Pueblo belief system, the dead have the power to help the living. The men take Teofilo to the village, where a traditional Pueblo funeral is held. But when the reservation's young Catholic priest, Father Paul, learns that Teofilo did not receive his "last rites" as ordered by the Catholic Church, he is angered and feels **insulted**. But later, when he is invited to sprinkle holy water on Teofilo's grave, he …

[3]   The great Native-American scholar and novelist Louis Owens once described this story much better than I can, so here he is: "Silko presents a Pueblo world with simple and profound clarity—no sentimental posturing, no romantic lens filtering. She expects us to enter that world the same way that the priest in the story does, through an **accommodation** made with understanding and respect. She allows feeling to displace the need for **empirical** knowledge. Silko makes us, above all, feel this world."

Notes   impoverished 「貧しくなった」   tended 「面倒を見た」   posturing 「気取った態度」

The Man to Send Rain Clouds ❖ Leslie Marmon Silko

▶ **Words in Context** Find the words in bold in the essay that match the definitions/synonyms below. Write the words on the lines.

1. _____ based on fact or scientific observation, not theory
2. _____ a give-and-take action; a fitting in or adaptation
3. _____ without guilt, regret, or a feeling of having done wrong
4. _____ native to an area or environment
5. _____ offended; disrespected; slighted
6. _____ in a way that seems true, but isn't; supposedly

▶ **Reading for Details** Write the requested information about "The Man to Send Rain Clouds" on the lines. Listen to check your answers. *T-CD 3-7*

1. _____ Silko's three ancestral roots
2. _____ where the story is set
3. _____ what life on the reservations can be like
4. _____ what Teofilo's job was
5. _____ what the two men asked of their dead grandfather
6. _____ what Teofilo's funeral did not include
7. _____ what Father Paul is later invited to do
8. _____ Louis Owens's "profile"

▶ **Making Conversation** With a partner, complete the conversation below. Listen to check and correct your answers. Then practice the conversation together. *T-CD 3-8*

A: What did white men take away from the indigenous people?

B: They _____.

A: What does the underlined word "surviving" in paragraph 1 imply?

B: It suggests that _____.

A: Why do the two men paint Teofilo's face and put a feather in his hair?

B: They are _____.

A: What does Louis Owens suggest about what Father Paul does?

B: He implies that Father Paul comes to _____.

49

Lesson 23

Are These Actual Miles? (1972)
Raymond Carver (American)

©GettyImages

 Reading *Read and listen to this short essay and then do the exercises that follow.*

[1] I almost met Raymond Carver once, in 1986, in Port Angeles, Washington, the town where he spent the last years of his life and I happened to be living. One day I went into the local bookshop to buy Carver's latest story collection. As I paid, the clerk said, "Mr. Carver was just here. You just missed him." I was disappointed but **curious**. "What did he buy?" I asked. "*The Tales of Anton Chekhov*, all 13 volumes," she said. "To re-read and re-study, he told me." Carver was then at the height of his reputation, **lauded** as the American equivalent of the great Russian short-story writer and playwright. And Carver was still learning from him!

[2] "Are These Actual Miles?" neatly illustrates what Carver described as his literary mission: "the gradual accretion of meaningful detail, the concrete word as opposed to the **abstract** or **arbitrary** or slippery word." In this story, every word, every detail matters. A married couple, Leo and Toni, are **ruined** financially. It's Saturday and they are scheduled to appear in **bankruptcy** court on Monday. They have a big, beautiful, American convertible that someone "might slap a lien on." So they need to sell the car—tonight. Toni is smart, good-looking, sexy. Charismatic. She'll get the most cash for the car. Leo watches anxiously as she puts on her make-up, does her hair, getting ready to "try" the city's car dealerships. And off she drives. Later, Leo waits even more anxiously for her to call and tell him that everything is OK, that they got the money. But she doesn't call … and doesn't call.

[3] About writing Chekhov once said, "Don't tell me the moon is shining; show me the glint of light on broken glass." Carver always took Chekhov's advice to heart. At the end of "Are These Actual Miles?" he doesn't tell us how broke and unhappy, Leo and Toni are, how their dreams have vanished. Instead, he simply shows us Leo standing in front of his house watching that big, shiny car—driven by another man—slowly disappear down the street. That car means everything.

Notes equivalent「対等なもの」　accretion「増大」　took ... to heart「心に刻む」

Are These Actual Miles? ❖ *Raymond Carver*

▶ Words in Context

Find the words in bold in the essay that match the definitions/synonyms below. Write the words on the lines.

1. _____ destroyed; completely spoiled
2. _____ eager to know about; very interested in
3. _____ being unable to pay one's debts
4. _____ not concrete or physical; conceptual; theoretical
5. _____ praised; recognized; hailed; admired
6. _____ random; not meaningful; unreasonable

▶ Reading for Details

Write the requested information about "Are These Actual Miles?" on the lines. Listen to check your answers. *T-CD 3-12*

1. _____ what Carver did in Port Angeles
2. _____ what Carver bought at the bookshop
3. _____ who Anton Chekhov was
4. _____ what "Are These Actual Miles" illustrates
5. _____ what will happen to Leo and Toni on Monday
6. _____ a legal word that means "security for payment"
7. _____ where Toni will try to sell the car
8. _____ what Leo waits for Toni to do

▶ Making Conversation

With a partner, complete the conversation below. Listen to check and correct your answers. Then practice the conversation together. *T-CD 3-13*

A: What was Carver planning to do with his bookshop purchase?

B: He was going to _____.

A: What did Carver imply by the underlined word "slippery"?

B: He most likely meant that some words _____.

A: What made Toni the better person for the job of selling the car?

B: She was _____.

A: What does Raymond Carver show us at the end of the story?

B: He shows us _____.

51

Lesson 24

A Loaf of Bread (1972)
James Alan McPherson (American)

©GettyImages

 Reading *Read and listen to this short essay and then do the exercises that follow.*

[1]   The contemporary African-American author ZZ Packer has said that although James Alan McPherson's stories may be about the lives of African-Americans, "they open out and give you a sense of what it means to be human." No story does this better than "A Loaf of Bread." It deals with racial discrimination and social injustice—with the lives of African-Americans—not by preaching or **overt** social commentary, but by deftly dramatizing the very "human" conflict of two men on opposite sides of the racial divide.

[2]   The story begins: "A grocer named Harold Green was caught red-handed selling to one group of people the very same goods he sold at lower prices at similar outlets in better neighborhoods." When Green's black customers learn how he has been **exploiting** them, they revolt. Led by a factory worker named Nelson Reed, they picket Green's store. Harold, baffled by the "**outrage** heaped on him," tells his wife Ruth, "I am not a dishonest man. I did not make this world. I only make my way in it." But Ruth's not satisfied. To "fix" the situation, she says that Harold must one day this week give away free anything his customers come in to buy. If he doesn't comply, she threatens, "You have seen the last of your children and myself."

[3]   Harold is adamant: "I will not knuckle under!" But the crisis **escalates**. Green and Reed meet in a coffee shop to try to work things out. Harold asks Nelson to "step into his shoes," to try to see how hard it is to run a profitable business. Nelson doesn't buy it: "Ain't no use to hide. I know you wrong, you know you wrong. Man, why you want to do people that way? We human, same as you." And then …

[4]   To me, McPherson's great story is a study of "free" in all its **connotations**. There's the practical "free," as in no charge. But also "free" as in liberated, no longer victimized. And "free" as in free of moral guilt. As in **redemption**.

Notes　**red-handed**「現行犯で」　　**comply**「応じる」　　**adamant**「譲らない」

A Loaf of Bread ◆ James Alan McPherson

Words in Context
Find the words in bold in the essay that match the definitions/synonyms below. Write the words on the lines.

1. _____ words' suggested or unspoken meanings
2. _____ anger; ire; fury; wrath
3. _____ gets larger; becomes more serious; worsens
4. _____ open; frank; blatant
5. _____ the state of being free of sin or guilt; absolution
6. _____ using in an unfair way; taking ill advantage of

Reading for Details
Write the requested information about "A Loaf of Bread" on the lines. Listen to check your answers. T-CD 3-17

1. _____ who ZZ Packer is
2. _____ who Harold Green is
3. _____ where Harold sold goods more cheaply
4. _____ Nelson Reed's occupation
5. _____ a word that means "demonstrate in protest"
6. _____ what Harold insists that he is NOT
7. _____ what Harold wants Nelson to try to do
8. _____ what Nelson says Harold knows

Making Conversation
With a partner, complete the conversation below. Listen to check and correct your answers. Then practice the conversation together. T-CD 3-18

A: What are the two main themes of "A Loaf of Bread"?

B: It deals with _____.

A: How does the story deal with these themes?

B: It does so by _____.

A: What does Harold Green say about the world?

B: He says that _____.

A: What does Nelson Reed say about Harold's customers?

B: He says that they _____.

Lesson 25

The Ones Who Walk Away from Omelas (1975)
Ursula K. Le Guin (American)

©Gorthian

Reading *Read and listen to this short essay and then do the exercises that follow.*

[1]   Ursula K. Le Guin, who died in 2018, was the author of *The Left Hand of Darkness* and *Earthsea*, two classic works of science fiction. But she always disliked being labeled a mere genre writer: "I get prickly if I'm called *just* a sci-fi writer. I'm not. I'm a novelist and a poet. Don't shove me into your pigeonhole, where I don't fit. My tentacles are coming out of the pigeonhole in all directions."

[2]   Some of those tentacles created "The Ones Who Walk Away from Omelas," a brief tale that is part sci-fi, part fantasy, part fairytale. But most of all, it is a kind of parable (or, as Le Guin called it, a "psychomyth") that critiques a disturbing **paradox** of contemporary civilization. The story opens at the annual summer celebration of the city of Omelas. And there is much to celebrate. Omelas is a magical, idyllic place—its architecture noble, its music **poignant**, its science profound, its harvests **abundant**, its citizens "mature, intelligent, passionate adults," its children healthy and happy.

[3]   But there's a catch. All this "good" depends on the existence of a child, locked in a dark, dank basement, who lives in "**abominable** misery"—whose life is one of fear, malnutrition, filth, and lonely neglect. "If this child were brought up into the sunlight out of that vile place, if it were cleaned and fed … in that day and hour all the prosperity and beauty and delight of Omelas would wither and disappear." The terms for this trade-off are strict and absolute. "There may not even be a kind word spoken to the child." But some Omelas citizens … well, read the story and see.

[4]   "The Ones Who Walk Away from Omelas" challenges our sense of social justice, our essential morality. Or, as David Brooks, a *New York Times* columnist, nicely put it: "This story rivets people because it confronts them with all the tragic **compromises** built into modern life—all the children in the basements—and, at the same time, **elicits** some desire to struggle against blandly accepting that condition."

Notes   parable「寓話」   idyllic「牧歌的な」   blandly「平然と」

Words in Context

Find the words in bold in the essay that match the definitions/synonyms below. Write the words on the lines.

1. _____ a statement that sounds absurd, but is actually true
2. _____ draws or brings out; makes happen; prompts; inspires
3. _____ existing in large quantities; plentiful
4. _____ truly bad or horrible; wretched; vile; dreadful
5. _____ understandings; agreements; settlements; deals
6. _____ touching; moving; affecting

Reading for Details

Write the requested information about "The Ones Who Walk Away from Omelas" on the lines. Listen to check your answers. *T-CD 3-22*

1. _____ two Ursula Le Guin science-fiction classics
2. _____ a word that means "narrow category or slot"
3. _____ how Le Guin saw her "Omelas" story
4. _____ what the story of Omelas critiques
5. _____ a slang word for a problem or drawback
6. _____ how the child in the basement lives
7. _____ what may not be spoken to the child
8. _____ who David Brooks is

Making Conversation

With a partner, complete the conversation below. Listen to check and correct your answers. Then practice the conversation together. *T-CD 3-23*

A: What kind of writer does Ursula K. Le Guin see herself as?

B: She's not *just* a sci-fi writer but _____.

A: How does the essay's author describe Le Guin's brief tale about Omelas?

B: He says that it is _____.

A: Why does Omelas have so much to celebrate?

B: Because it is a _____.

A: What desire does David Brooks say the story brings out in people?

B: It brings out our desire to struggle against _____.

Lesson 26

Bobby's Room (1984)
Douglas Dunn (Scottish)

Reading *Read and listen to this short essay and then do the exercises that follow.*

[1]   The great British poet Philip Larkin once wrote: "They fuck you up, your mum and dad, they don't mean to but they do. They fill you with the faults they had, and add some extra just for you." I was reminded of these darkly humorous lines while reading "Bobby's Room," a bildungsroman about a Scottish teenager named Henry Pollock. Henry is an only child whose **negligent**, self-absorbed parents are—blithely—"messing" Henry up. But in Henry's case, the parents' faults don't "take." Unlike in Larkin's gloomy view, here, there's room for hope.

[2]   And all thanks to a rashly selfish act. Mr. and Mrs. Pollock fly off to Singapore for three months, leaving Henry behind at an inn run by a Mrs. Bawden. Henry, nearly in tears over this abandonment, wonders "why they could continue to be so ignorant of his feelings." But then Henry, characteristically **reticent**, decides "not to make it difficult for them and resigns himself to his plight."

[3]   Mrs. Bawden puts Henry up in her son Bobby's room. Bobby, another only child, is grown up and long gone. But the more Henry gets to know Mrs. Bawden, the more he **identifies** with Bobby. He sometimes even imagines that Bobby is there in "Bobby's room" with him, helping Henry "deal with circumstances."

[4]   How Henry handles these circumstances is to simply pitch in at the inn. "As the days went by he found himself aproned, pulling linens from beds, vacuuming carpets, dusting furniture, cleaning windows and mirrors, waiting tables."

[5]   One guest is a bored, **petulant** girl named Louise. She's Henry's age and also the only child of selfish, neglectful parents. Louise **inadvertently** helps Henry cope and mature. "Looking at her, Henry thought there might be two major ways in which only children could turn out: they became either super-obliging, obedient models of courtesy and good behaviour or, like Louise, rebelliously surly and aggrieved. Henry never allowed his own **grievances** to show, and doubted if he ever would." But then Henry … well, let's just say that he finds his own way.

Notes   **"take"**「奪い去る」   **abandonment**「見捨てられること」
         resigns himself to「自らやめる」

Words in Context

Find the words in bold in the essay that match the definitions/synonyms below. Write the words on the lines.

1. _____ without knowing or being aware; unintentionally
2. _____ complaints; resentments; ill-feelings
3. _____ not paying attention; careless; thoughtless; irresponsible
4. _____ feels close to; shares the feelings of; feels similar to
5. _____ not saying much; quiet; taciturn
6. _____ having a bad attitude; bad-tempered; sulky

Reading for Details

Write the requested information about "Bobby's Room" on the lines. Listen to check your answers. 3-27

1. _____ what Larkin says parents fill their children with
2. _____ how the lines from Larkin's poem are described
3. _____ Henry's parents' rashly selfish act
4. _____ what kind of establishment Mrs. Bawden runs
5. _____ a word meaning "a difficult situation"
6. _____ where Bobby is now
7. _____ an idiom meaning "to help out" or "lend a hand"
8. _____ what some of Henry's chores are

Making Conversation

With a partner, complete the conversation below. Listen to check and correct your answers. Then practice the conversation together. 3-28

A: Why does the essay's author say that there is room for hope in Henry?

B: Because Henry's parents' _____.

A: What does Henry's parents' abandonment make Henry feel and wonder?

B: He wonders _____.

A: How are Henry and Louise similar?

B: They both _____.

A: What kind of person does Henry see himself as?

B: He believes that he _____.

Lesson 27

The Things They Carried (1986)
Tim O'Brien (American)

©Larry D. Moor

Reading *Read and listen to this short essay and then do the exercises that follow.*

[1]   In literature, a tragedy is a story in which the protagonist meets his downfall because of a "fatal flaw"—a moral weakness or inability to cope with **adversity**. The Vietnam War, which the United States fought for nearly two decades and **ultimately** lost (resulting in the deaths of over three million people on both sides of the conflict), has been called a tragedy in this sense, with America being the main character, and its tragic flaw being … greed, arrogance, **ignorance**, lust for power, paranoia—you name it. "The Things They Carried" powerfully dramatizes this tragedy, which features a storytelling technique of **stunning** originality. Tim O'Brien served in Vietnam, from 1969 to 1970, and based his story on firsthand experience.

[2]   The plot is minimal. Lieutenant Jimmy Cross is the 22-year-old leader of a small platoon of American "grunts" on a mission to seek and destroy the Viet Cong enemy. Jimmy isn't a very dependable leader. He distracts himself from his appalling circumstances by fantasizing about a girl back home. But then something terrible happens, and Jimmy feels responsible. This wrenches him back into reality. "There was a new hardness in his stomach. He was now determined to perform his duties firmly, without negligence," the narrator tells us. And that's about it for plot.

[3]   But the "real" story, as its title suggests, is in the things that the 17 men in Jimmy's platoon carry. The narrator matter-of-factly, dispassionately categorizes them—tangible things like rifles, ammunition, foot powder, chewing gum, photographs. But Jimmy's men also "carry" Vietnam itself—"The whole atmosphere, the humidity, the monsoons, the stink of fungus and decay." They carry themselves, too, some with a "**wistful** resignation," others with "pride and stiff soldierly discipline or good humor or macho **zeal**." But most of all, they carry the "emotional baggage of men who might die—grief, terror, love, longing." Near the story's end, Jimmy Cross thinks, "It was very sad. The things men carried inside. The things men did or felt they had to do." Tragic, really.

Notes paranoia 「疑心暗鬼」   dispassionately 「冷静に」   ammunition 「弾薬」

Words in Context

Find the words in bold in the essay that match the definitions/synonyms below. Write the words on the lines.

1. _____ lack of knowledge; inexperience; innocence
2. _____ enthusiasm; eagerness; passion; ardor
3. _____ difficulty; trouble; an unpleasant situation
4. _____ in the end; in the final analysis; eventually
5. _____ very noticeable; striking; very impressive; superb
6. _____ having a feeling of vague longing; dreamy; pensive

Reading for Details

Write the requested information about "The Things They Carried" on the lines. Listen to check your answers.

1. _____ a word that means "ruin, defeat, end, failure"
2. _____ how long America was involved in Vietnam
3. _____ what Tim O'Brien based his story on
4. _____ a slang expression for "foot soldier"
5. _____ how Jimmy Cross distracts himself
6. _____ what Jimmy felt in his stomach
7. _____ five tangible things the men carried
8. _____ the men's "emotional baggage"

Making Conversation

With a partner, complete the conversation below. Listen to check and correct your answers. Then practice the conversation together.

A: What makes a work of literature a "tragedy"?

B: A story is a tragedy when _____.

A: What feature makes "The Things They Carried" so striking?

B: Its storytelling _____.

A: What happens after Jimmy Cross is forced to face reality?

B: He becomes more responsible, _____.

A: How does the author of the essay describe the story's narrative voice?

B: He calls it _____.

Lesson **28**

The Management of Grief (1988)
Bharati Mukherjee (Indian-American)

 3-36 ▶ **Reading** *Read and listen to this short essay and then do the exercises that follow.*

[1]   From its title, you might think "The Management of Grief" depressing. And it could be. It centers around a real-life tragedy—the 1985 crash of Air India Flight 182 into the Atlantic Ocean off the coast of Ireland. All 329 people on board—many of them Indians or of Indian descent—were killed. Investigators later determined that Sikh militants had planted a bomb in the plane's luggage hold.

[2]   And yet, through a miracle of narrative art, the story isn't depressing—sad, yes, but not depressing. We come away from reading it inspired, enlightened, **fortified** thanks to the remarkably humane voice of the narrator, Shaila Bhave, an Indian immigrant to Canada who has just suffered an **unspeakable** loss: Her husband and two young sons were on Flight 182. The story begins in Mrs. Bhave's house, where friends and neighbors have gathered to **console** her, "whispering and moving **tactfully**," Mrs. Bhave tells us.

[3]   Shaila travels to Ireland to identify her husband's and sons' bodies, though they are never recovered. She then flies to India to stay with her parents and undergo traditional Hindu **rituals** of mourning. But then, despite objections from her family, Shaila returns to Canada to **resume** her life there. She keeps in touch with other family survivors like herself and assists a social worker, Judith, who is helping the "hysterical relatives" of some crash victims. "Judith sees me as calm and accepting," Shaila tells the reader, "but worries that I have no job, no career. My closest friends are worse off than I. I cannot tell Judith that my days, even my nights, are thrilling."

[4]   Thrilling? An odd word to connect with grief. But that's the thing about Shaila; she manages things differently, uniquely going beyond "textbook" notions of the stages of "grief management"—rejection, depression, acceptance, reconstruction—to begin her own "voyage" and to find her own "direction." And Shaila's "management of grief," writes the American author Richard Ford, "also becomes the story's means of assuring readers that grief can be withstood."

Notes   militants 「過激派」   mourning 「喪に服すこと」

Words in Context

Find the words in bold in the essay that match the definitions/synonyms below. Write the words on the lines.

1. _____ thoughtfully; sensitively; carefully; politely
2. _____ start where one left off; begin again; carry on with
3. _____ strengthened; emboldened; enabled
4. _____ so sad or bad as to be inexpressible in words
5. _____ comfort someone in a time of trouble; support
6. _____ ceremonies; practices; customs

Reading for Details

Write the requested information about "The Management of Grief" on the lines. Listen to check your answers. T-CD 3-37

1. _____ where Flight 182 crashed
2. _____ why it crashed
3. _____ who Shaila Bhave is
4. _____ who has gathered in Shaila's house
5. _____ why Shaila travels to Ireland
6. _____ with whom Shaila stays in India
7. _____ Judith's profession
8. _____ how Shaila refers to her life from now on

Making Conversation

With a partner, complete the conversation below. Listen to check and correct your answers. Then practice the conversation together. T-CD 3-38

A: Why might we think "The Management of Grief" depressing?

B: Because of its title and also because _____.

A: Was Shaila able to identify her husband's and sons' bodies?

B: No, because _____.

A: Why is Shaila "different"?

B: Because she goes beyond _____.

A: What does Richard Ford say the story does for readers?

B: He says that it _____.

Lesson 29

The Bear Came Over the Mountain (1999)
Alice Munro (Canadian)

 Reading *Read and listen to this short essay and then do the exercises that follow.*

[1]   When Alice Munro won the 2013 Nobel Prize for Literature, writers everywhere were **jubilant**. A "writer's writer," Munro, through her work, inspires and instructs other authors, both **aspiring** and veteran. The fine American short-story writer Jhumpa Lahiri says that it was Munro who taught her what a short story can do. "Alice turned the form on its head," Lahiri wrote.

[2]   Most Munro stories are set in rural Canada, and many deal with the vicissitudes of marriage and family life. Each is so packed with **incident**, information, and insight that it reads like a 300-page novel. The English writer Julian Barnes is another Munro admirer: "Alice can move characters through time like no other writer. You are not aware that time is passing, only that it has passed. In this, the reader resembles the characters, who also find that time has passed, that their lives have been changed, without their quite understanding how, where, and why."

[3]   That's "The Bear Came Over the Mountain" to a T. The story's action starts decades ago, when the two main characters, Grant and Fiona, meet, fall in love, get married. Jump ahead 45 years to the present, and it's the day Grant is driving Fiona to Meadowlake, a nursing home for Alzheimer's sufferers. We then flash back two years to when Fiona's mind and memory first start to wander—to when she often wanders off and gets lost herself. Then we jump ahead again to a month after Fiona's admission to Meadowlake. Because of a nursing-home rule, Grant has been **banned** from visiting his wife for 30 days, and has been **frantically** worried about her. Now, finally, he goes to Meadowlake only to find that Fiona has formed a strong romantic **bond** with a man named Aubrey, a fellow patient. Fiona looks at Grant and wonders ... Do I know you? And then ...

[4]   Another contemporary author, Roxana Robinson, puts Munro's greatness like this: "Alice never sets out to make a political point. She has no axe to grind. She's simply bearing witness to the human experience, reporting from the front lines."

Notes   wander 「さまよう」   "bearing witness to" 「証言している」

The Bear Came Over the Mountain ❖ Alice Munro

▶ Words in Context
Find the words in bold in the essay that match the definitions/synonyms below. Write the words on the lines.

1. _____ event; happening; occurrence
2. _____ prevented from doing; forbidden; excluded
3. _____ relationship; connection; attachment
4. _____ very happy; ecstatic; elated
5. _____ desperately; in a panic-stricken way; filled with worry
6. _____ hopeful; prospective; potential

▶ Reading for Details
Write the requested information about "The Bear Came Over the Mountain" on the lines. Listen to check your answers. 🎧 T-CD 3-42

1. _____ what happened in 2013
2. _____ what Alice Munro taught Jhumpa Lahiri
3. _____ a big word that means "life's ups and downs"
4. _____ what many Alice Munro stories read like
5. _____ when "The Bear Came Over the Mountain" starts
6. _____ what Meadowlake is
7. _____ for how long Grant has not seen Fiona
8. _____ an idiomatic expression that means "having no selfish aims or goals"

▶ Making Conversation
With a partner, complete the conversation below. Listen to check and correct your answers. Then practice the conversation together. 🎧 T-CD 3-43

A: Why is Alice Munro called a "writer's writer"?

B: Because her work _____.

A: What does Jhumpa Lahiri most likely mean by "Alice turned the form on its head"?

B: She probably means that Alice Munro _____.

A: What most impresses Julian Barnes about Munro's work?

B: He admires how _____.

A: What shocked Grant when he first visited Fiona in Meadowlake?

B: He found that _____.

Lesson 30

Saboteur (2000)
Ha Jin (Chinese-American)

©GettyImages

 Reading *Read and listen to this short essay and then do the exercises that follow.*

[1]   Anton Chekhov, the great Russian writer I've mentioned before, once said: "If in the first act you have hung a pistol on the wall, then in the following act it should be fired. Otherwise, don't put the gun there." This concept, "Chekhov's Gun," has long served as a lesson for creative writers. Simply put, it implies that a story must be **cohesive**. All the parts must contribute effectively to the whole.

[2]   In "Saboteur," Ha Jin honors Chekhov's advice by following it faithfully. He introduces the "gun" early on in this way: "During the two weeks' vacation, [Mr. Chiu] had been worried about his liver, because three months ago, he had suffered from acute hepatitis; he was afraid he might have a relapse." The "gun" in this case, then, is hepatitis, and it is "fired" later on in an unexpected, **disconcerting** way.

[3]   Mr. Chiu and his new bride are having lunch at a cafe on the last day of their honeymoon. Suddenly, a "stout, middle-aged" policeman at a nearby table tosses tea at them. Mr. Chiu protests: "Comrade Policeman, why did you do this?" The policeman denies it. "Do what?" he says. Mr. Chiu loses his temper and **chastises** him: "Your duty is to keep order, but you purposely tortured us as citizens. Why **violate** the law you are supposed to enforce?" The policeman then accuses Mr. Chiu of sabotage, handcuffs him, and marches him off to jail. Mr. Chiu's wife is left behind, sobbing. And then …

[4]   Ha Jin studied English in China before going to the United States in 1984 to get his Ph.D. at Brandeis University. He intended to return home to China to teach, but then came the 1989 Tiananmen Square incident in Beijing, when the Chinese government brutally suppressed a student rebellion. The government's action outraged him, and Ha Jin decided not to return to China—to stay in America and write exclusively in English. "Saboteur," with its themes of **corruption** and injustice, dramatizes and **epitomizes** the author's—and his protagonist's—anger and vengefulness.

Notes   stout「頑強な」   tortured = "were very cruel to"「ひどく苦しめる」
handcuffs「手錠をかける」   suppressed「鎮圧した」   exclusively「もっぱら」

Words in Context

Find the words in bold in the essay that match the definitions/synonyms below. Write the words on the lines.

1. _____ serves as an example; sums up; embodies
2. _____ upsetting; disturbing; unsettling
3. _____ dishonest or illegal behavior; misconduct
4. _____ disobey; break; breach; flout
5. _____ scolds; criticizes angrily; tells off in a very severe way
6. _____ held together in a uniform way; united; consistent

Reading for Details

Write the requested information about "Saboteur" on the lines. Listen to check your answers. T-CD 3-47

1. _____ another word for gun or handgun
2. _____ what Chekhov is referring to by the word "act"
3. _____ what organ the disease hepatitis affects
4. _____ a word that means "the return of an illness"
5. _____ what Mr. Chiu and his wife have been celebrating
6. _____ how the policeman is described
7. _____ what Mr. Chiu is charged with or accused of
8. _____ what happened in 1989

Making Conversation

With a partner, complete the conversation below. Listen to check and correct your answers. Then practice the conversation together. T-CD 3-48

A: What kind of lesson has "Chekhov's Gun" taught writers?

B: It has taught them that _____.

A: How did Ha Jin "honor" Chekhov's advice or lesson?

B: He did so _____.

A: What does Mr. Chiu say is a policeman's duty?

B: He says that his duty _____.

A: What do Mr. Chiu and Ha Jin have in common?

B: They both _____.

著作権法上、無断複写・複製は禁じられています。

Top 30: Essential Short Stories in English: 1843 to 2000　　[B-875]
大学生が読むべき世界の短編 30

1　刷　　2019 年 4 月 1 日

著　者　　Jim Knudsen

発行者　　南雲　一範　Kazunori Nagumo
発行所　　株式会社　南雲堂
　　　　　〒162-0801　東京都新宿区山吹町361
　　　　　NAN'UN-DO Co., Ltd.
　　　　　361 Yamabuki-cho, Shinjuku-ku, Tokyo 162-0801, Japan
　　　　　振替口座：00160-0-46863
　　　　　TEL：　03-3268-2311（営業部：学校関係）
　　　　　　　　 03-3268-2384（営業部：書店関係）
　　　　　　　　 03-3268-2387（編集部）
　　　　　FAX：　03-3269-2486
編集者　　加藤　敦

組　版　　柴崎　利恵

装　丁　　銀　月　堂

検　印　　省　略

コード　　ISBN978-4-523-17875-0　C0082

　　　　　　　　　　　　　　　　　　　Printed in Japan

E-mail : nanundo@post.email.ne.jp
URL : http://www.nanun-do.co.jp/